One Unt

The Life and Ministry
of the Apostle Paul

One Untimely Born
The Life and Ministry of the Apostle Paul

by
ROBERT L. CATE

MERCER
UNIVERSITY PRESS

ISBN 0-86554-995-8   MUP/P329

Library of Congress Cataloging-in-Publication Data

Cate, Robert L.
    One untimely born : the life and ministry of the Apostle Paul /
by Robert L. Cate. -- 1st ed.
        p.   cm.
    Includes bibliographical references and index.
ISBN-13: 978-0-86554-995-1 (pbk. : alk. paper)
ISBN-10: 0-86554-995-8 (pbk. : alk. paper)
    1. Paul, the Apostle, Saint.   2. Christian saints--Turkey--Tarsus
--Biography. 3. Tarsus (Turkey)--Biography. 4. Bible. N.T. --Biography.
    I. Title.
BS2506.3.C38 2006
225.9'2--dc22
    [B]

                                                    2006013452

Contents

To Dot,

my partner in this as in everything.

Love never ends.

(First Corinthians 13:8)

Foreword

One Untimely Born: The Life and Ministry of the Apostle Paul was more than twenty-five years in the making. This was uncharacteristic of my father's writing. His thirteen other books were executed with almost military precision. Dad would develop an idea for a book, draft an outline listing the number of pages and target completion date for each chapter, and then finish the book on or before the due date—never more than a year after beginning work—and within a page or two of his original prediction. He was a publisher's dream.

This book was different. First contemplated in 1980 while on sabbatical at Oxford, writing was not begun until the 1990s and then took fifteen years to complete. Many factors contributed to the extended timing, including work on other projects, but two were most important. The first had to do with the nature of the subject. The Apostle Paul is arguably the most important figure, other than Jesus himself, in the history of the early church and the development of Christian theology. He is the subject of thousands of books and articles, with more being written every year. More than a third of the New Testament is by, dedicated to, or about Paul. To write credibly about Paul requires mastering a vast, diverse, and constantly expanding body of material. It is a life's work. Therefore it is not surprising that it took a good part of Dad's professional life to complete it.

The second reason concerns the nature of the book. More than any other book I saw Dad undertake, this one reflects on his own spiritual and intellectual pilgrimage as a pastor, teacher, and author. It describes the foundations of Christian faith that he dedicated his entire adult life to preaching, teaching, and writing about. While demonstrating the characteristics for which Dad's work has always been known—rigorous, intellectually honest scholarship conveyed in accessible terms with clarity and conviction—it is at the same time intensely personal. For this reason too, this study of Paul took some time to finish.

The time in process, the importance of the subject, and the personal nature of the quest all lend poignancy to the fact that *One Untimely Born* is Dad's last book. He died while the book was in press, after a long and courageous fight with a progressive neurological disease. Finishing this book was a—perhaps *the*—major preoccupation of Dad's final days. As disease robbed him of the ability to frequent libraries and use a keyboard, I, aided by other members of the family, helped to track down sources and reconcile drafts. This provided me with an unparalleled opportunity to work closely with Dad and to witness firsthand his expansive knowledge, his insight, and the clarity of his thinking and expression. I will always treasure that experience.

Publishing a book by an author who will not be available to participate in the editorial and marketing processes is a risky undertaking. Dad was delighted when Mercer University Press, which had previously included twenty entries by him in its authoritative *Mercer Dictionary of the Bible*, agreed to undertake the task. Were he still alive, Dad would most certainly thank the Press, and especially Director Marc A. Jolley and Senior Editor Edmon L. Rowell, Jr., for their willingness to take on that risk and the additional work it surely created for them, and for their skill and professionalism throughout the publication process. I am honored to do so on his behalf, and on behalf of the entire family, I also thank them for their kindness and sensitivity.

Second only to his faith and his family, Dad valued most of all the students, church members, readers, and others for whom he sought to make the Bible alive and real. He believed that scholarship, conveyed in practical, understandable terms, was an essential foundation of faith, and that true Christian faith is strengthened, not compromised, by asking hard questions. Although this conviction has met with resistance in recent years, it was the cornerstone of his ministry and his life and is the basis for this book. It is therefore fitting that Dad's final work should explore for the lay reader the life and ministry of a man so important to Christian faith but so often out of sync with his own time that he described himself as "one untimely born."

Fred H. Cate

Preface

Those familiar with my writings may well ask why one who has devoted a major portion his life to the study of the Old Testament is writing a book about one of the central figures of the New Testament. A legitimate question, this surely deserves a serious answer.

For more than fifty years my primary commitment to biblical study has been to make the Bible, the whole Bible, come to life for those who read it. This means that I am and have always been concerned with all of the Bible, not just with the Old Testament. Although my primary field of study over the years has indeed been the Old Testament, my study there has been devoted to and directed by the concern and the belief that knowledge of the Old Testament is a vital key to understanding the New Testament. In fact, knowledge of the Old Testament is a necessary foundation for one to be able even to begin the process of interpreting the New Testament.

Furthermore, while a significant part of my life has been devoted to the study of the Old Testament, my major focus has always been proclaiming the Gospel of Jesus Christ. Because of this, two major areas of my biblical studies have been the New Testament in general and in particular the life of Jesus. This interest and concern has been reflected in at least three of my books: *A History of the New Testament and Its Times*, *A History of the Bible Lands in the Interbiblical Period*, and *Help in Ages Past, Hope for Years to Come*. Thus my study and research in the past has regularly and consistently expanded into the field of the New Testament.

Over the years I have also devoted myself to the study of Paul and his writings. One of the greatest missionaries who ever lived, Paul was arguably the early church's most significant representative. For good or ill, a major part of Christianity's understanding of the mission of Jesus has been shaped by the writings and influence of this one man and his companions in mission and ministry. Some have even gone so far as to suggest that he is so influential that he has led the church to misunderstand Jesus as well as its own nature and mission.

My personal interest in Paul was whetted significantly by the lectures of the late Professor George Caird, principal of Mansfield College, Oxford University, during a year of sabbatical study in 1980–1981. Over a period of two terms, he led an ever-enlarging group of students in considering "The Quest for the Historical Paul." Professor Caird stimulated my mind, touched my heart, and altered my life. Unfortunately, his untimely death prevented the final summation of his thoughts on that subject from ever getting into print.

Challenged by the thoughts and suggestions of Professor Caird, I have spent a significant portion of time and energy in the intervening years studying and pondering the life and ministry of Paul, as well as trying to unravel some of the historical, theological, and psychological problems that surround this man and his life and ministry. The present work is the product of that study.

My purpose in writing this book is to introduce the inquiring, serious student of the Bible to the ministry of this great man who described himself in his relationship to the Lord Jesus Christ as "one untimely born" (1 Cor. 15:8 RSV). I also hope that those who are intimately familiar with the ministry of Paul as revealed in the Book of Acts and in Paul's epistles will find in these pages both a stimulating review as well as a source of occasional food for thought.

To avoid distraction, I have sought to keep footnotes to a minimum. Those fully familiar with the subject will recognize my indebtedness to many who have gone before in this area of biblical study. I make no claim to have read all the works of those scholars who have probed into Paul's life and ministry. I do believe I have become familiar with the major approaches made by them and have studied them in detail where it seemed necessary and/or profitable. My study has led me to agree with some of these and to disagree with others. My disagreements in no way indicate that those with whom I disagree have not significantly stimulated my thinking or contributed to my knowledge. In fact, I am perhaps even more indebted to those with whom I have disagreed than to those with whom I have agreed. They have challenged me to examine the evidence more thoroughly and to think more deeply about the issues involved in my own spiritual and intellectual pilgrimage.

Anyone who reads this material deserves to know the relevant presuppositions with which I have approached this study. I clearly realize that my presuppositions, like those of anyone else who does such research, are intensely personal. Therefore it is hard for me to be objective about them. However, insofar as I have been able to analyze them and to understand their impact upon my study and writing, the following seem to me to be the most significant.

That God exists and that God has acted redemptively for humanity through the life and death of his son Jesus goes without question for me. Further, that I am a sinner, albeit a saved one, also goes without question. Both my sin and my experience have shown me that I can be wrong, both morally and intellectually. Therefore what I present here is set forth as my best conclusions at the present moment with no illusions about the fact that I have probably made some mistakes. If so, they are not my first. (It seems strange to me to hear some people who claim to believe that they are sinners and thus morally wrong, assume—or pretend?—that they could never be wrong intellectually.)

Another of my presuppositions which needs to be identified here is a negative one. Many people treat Paul in a manner that almost seems to put him on a level with Jesus Christ. Paul appears in many such treatments to be presented as almost semidivine. Admittedly, these authors make no such claim for him and would deny that they held such a view, but the manner in which they write or speak of him seems to leave this impression. To me such an approach is incredible. Paul was a human being and, according to his own admission, subject to the frailties of human flesh. God is infallible. Paul wasn't. However, he was a man who, to the best of his own abilities, was wholly devoted to the service of the Lord Jesus. No one can be more.

From the foundation of these presuppositions, I have studied the life of Paul for information as to his strengths and weaknesses, his accomplishments and failures, and his victories and defeats. I have also sought to understand Paul's character and mission against the background of the times in which he lived and of the personal influences that brought him into the service of the Lord Jesus Christ and kept him there to the end of his days. It is my hope and prayer that, as you join me in this study, you will find Paul at many points to be an example worthy to be copied. It is also my hope and prayer that when you have completed this study, you will at least have a better understanding of what it means to be a servant of the living Lord. Perhaps you will even put that understanding into your life, being or becoming a better Christian.

Join me, then, in the study of one whom I believe to have been one of greatest men who ever lived, a man who described himself as "one untimely born," the Apostle Paul.

Robert L. Cate

One Untimely Born

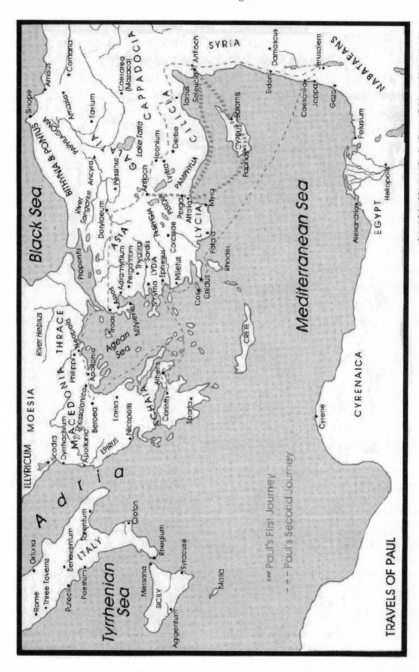

TRAVELS OF PAUL

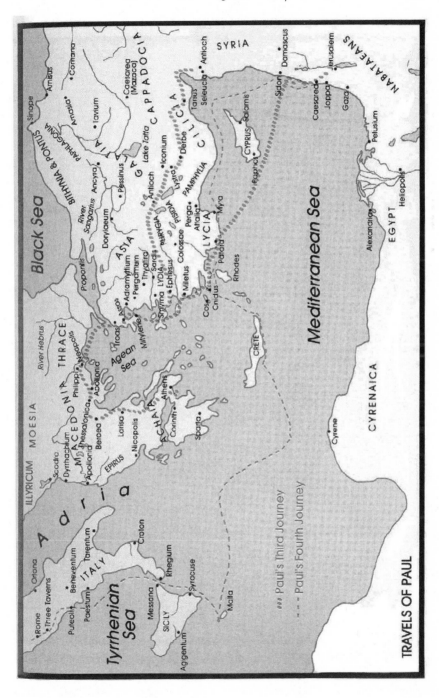

Chapter 1

Introductory Considerations

Few people in world history have truly earned the right to be called "great." When you focus the area of consideration upon the field of religion, this number becomes significantly less. And when that field is reduced to those persons involved in the founding of the Christian church, the number becomes almost negligible.

However, just because the number of "greats" in the history of the church is small, this in no way means that the significance of the church itself is small. To the contrary, we can find hope in the fact that, over the years, the major ministry of the church has been predominantly carried forward by people who were quite ordinary. Furthermore, that the church has been primarily served by very ordinary people should not prove surprising, for that was precisely the kind of people whom Jesus called to be his first disciples. Not one really "great" person was to be found among the collection of fishermen, tax collectors, and otherwise "uneducated, common" people whom Jesus gathered around him during his earthly ministry (Acts 4:13).

Yet the very fact that not one of those early disciples of Jesus stood out as being truly great is what makes the apostle Paul so striking. For he was *great* in every sense of the word and by almost every standard of measurement that might be applied. More than one-third of the New Testament is by, dedicated to, or about Paul. His memory has been preserved over the years by such phrases as "the great apostle" or "the apostle extraordinary."[1] This almost unique greatness of Paul is one of the things that has made him such a fascinating figure over the years and has given rise to so much study of his life and ministry.

Other Studies

Only a superficial glance at the bibliography of this book will reveal just how many studies of the life and ministry of Paul are readily available.

---

[1]Numerous authors have called Paul "the great apostle." Reginald E. O. White popularized the title of "apostle extraordinary." White, *Apostle Extraordinary* (Grand Rapids MI: Eerdmans, 1962). Maurice F. Wiles even dared to call him the "divine apostle." Wiles, *The Divine Apostle: The Interpretation of St. Paul's Epistles in the Early Church* (Cambridge: Cambridge University Press, 1967). Henrietta Buckmaster identified him as the "man who changed the world." Buckmaster, *Paul: A Man Who Changed the World* (New York: McGraw-Hill, 1965).

While I believe this list contains the best works that are at present easily available in English, they are only a small part of the total number of books that have been written to deal with the great apostle.

These studies on Paul vary from the merely sermonic to the extremely scholarly pieces of research which delve into the most esoteric aspects of Paul's life, ministry, and thought. Some are written in the form of popular biography while others deal in the most scientific manner with the minute details of chronological, theological, and historical problems. Some are written like a historical novel while others reflect the most serious historical investigation. And some probe into the details of the faith of the great apostle while others seek to consider his ethics and the application of that faith both to ancient and to modern problems. In fact, so varied and diverse are the studies about Paul that the student can find almost any approach to the life and ministry of the great apostle if the search is long and broad enough. That is both the blessing and the bane of student of the life and ministry of Paul.

Purposes of this Study

This overabundance of studies about Paul raises a fundamental question: if there are so many and so many different kinds of books about Paul, why is there any need for another? To put it another way, what is both different and valuable about this particular study when compared with others that are available for the student? The answer to this lies in my own goals and purposes for this study. Most of my goals can be found separately in other books, but I do not know of any single book that encompasses all of them.

The following list describes my goals in terms of what I am trying to accomplish with this study. In this book I am seeking

1. to analyze all of the available *biblical* evidence in an attempt to reconstruct and understand the life and ministry of the Apostle Paul;
2. to search through the known and relevant extrabiblical evidence of ancient contemporary historical and archaeological records for the light they may shed upon the life and ministry of the Apostle Paul;
3. to give serious consideration to the best of modern scholarship in trying to understand and to reconstruct the life and ministry of Paul;
4. to present a reconstruction of the life and ministry of Paul in *simple* terms so that the beginning student can comprehend the issues involved

and understand the major differences between the facts considered and the theories that have been created to explain those facts;

5. to keep reference notes to a minimum so that beginning students will not be distracted, while giving sufficient bibliographical references in order that a serious inquiry may be made by those who wish to pursue any part of the study further;

6. to help those who are already familiar with the subject and its basic issues to review and rethink them;

7. to try to understand the features of Paul's cultural and spiritual background which influenced his developing faith and ethics;

8. to come to grips with the unique features of Paul's faith and ministry, as well as to understand those common aspects which he shared with others of his day;

9. to seek to reconstruct the basic and primary issues of his faith and ethics while trying to understand how he carried these into the actual missions and ministries where he served and which he performed;

10. to try to perceive Paul as a human being who sought to devote his whole life and being to the service of the Gospel of the Lord Jesus Christ; and

11. to study the Pauline epistles with the purpose of understanding the man, his ministry, and his mission rather than here attempting to interpret and apply them to contemporary life.

The combination of and the relationship among these goals are what make this present work important. To deal with this material will surely demand a serious investment of time and energy by the reader. You will need to consider thoughtfully the evidence put forth and the conclusions drawn, and evaluate the biblical evidence for yourself. While I hope you will find this book informative and stimulating, it is not written as entertainment.

Sources for the Study

Any attempt to understand and/or reconstruct history, whether ancient or modern, depends upon at least four significant factors. The first is the quality of the primary sources the investigator has available. No historical investigation and reconstruction can ever be better than the quality of the sources available to the author. Further, in considering the quality of these sources from the historian's standpoint, our concern must be with their quality as historical documents, having no bearing upon their quality as faith statements.[2]

The second factor in historical research and reconstruction is the competence of the investigator. It matters little that the primary sources are of good quality and furnish abundant, accurate, and relevant information. If the one doing the investigating is incompetent, highly prejudiced, or even just not very skillful in accomplishing the task, the end result will be of little or no value. Competence in historical research and writing clearly relates to both training and experience. Training for historical investigation prepares one to do the job. Experience in doing historical investigation gives a maturity to the work which training alone can never supply.

The third factor which influences the quality of historical investigation and reconstruction depends upon the very "being" of the investigator. This clearly includes the presuppositions with which the task is approached by the historian and the intuitive insights that nature and experience have granted. This does not mean that a good historical investigator need be a genius, making massive leaps of intuitive insight. In fact, such genius may often be a hindrance to a good historian, for leaps of insight far too often are made at the expense of ignoring hard evidence. What this does mean is that such a person must have a healthy ability to see new relationships among old evidence. The historian without a good instinct to guide will frequently falter in the perceptiveness of the questions asked of the sources being used. When the basic questions asked of the primary documents are not good, then the answers found will not be of as great a value as they might otherwise have been.

The fourth factor, while not of the same level as the first three, is quite important nonetheless. This is *the investigator's familiarity with and understanding of the work of others who have gone before.* Only a fool plows over the same ground which has been plowed before unless there is

---

[2]Any historian using the works of Flavius Josephus, for example, must remember that Josephus's two primary purposes appear to have been to defend himself as a loyal Jew and to make Judaism acceptable to the Romans. Because of these motives, he sometimes tends to shape the evidence, or at least to pick and choose evidence that fulfills his purposes. This means that historians using his material as a source must use it with extreme caution.

In addition, the Book of Acts may be an excellent statement of the faith and proclamation of the early church, but if Luke were not a good historian or if he had any personally questionable motives for writing, its value as a primary source for the *history* of the early church becomes negligible.

reason to suppose that the former plowing either was not done properly or unless something new is to be added to the soil. In other words, a historian does not waste time covering the same material unless there is new evidence or a strong reason to believe that old evidence has in some way been misunderstood or inadequately dealt with, or the conclusions poorly communicated.

With these thoughts in mind, we are now ready to consider the sources that are available to us for the study of Paul's life and ministry. We are also ready to look at what some of the major modern interpreters have done with the evidence which these sources provide.

The Biblical Sources

The primary material available for the study of Paul's ministry is found in the Bible. Specifically, it is found in the Book of Acts and in the Pauline epistles.

The Book of Acts. No significant question exists but that Acts and Luke are by the same man. That being so, it is unlikely that the author's qualities as a historian would be different from one writing to the other of these. Thus evidence as to Luke's qualities as a historian in one can certainly be transposed to the other.

In his introduction to the Gospel, Luke claims to have been aware of and to have used many reliable sources (Luke 1:1-4). Most scholars agree that he was familiar with the four great centers of early Christianity: Jerusalem, Rome, Antioch, and Caesarea. It is also usually assumed that he was familiar with at least two written sources, the Gospel of Mark and a collection of Jesus' teachings sometimes identified by scholars as *Quelle* or Q, which was also apparently used by Matthew. In checking on how Luke used these sources, we discover he made few changes in what he found there. In other words, he appears to have been a careful historian in his use of the sources which he had. This allows us to conclude or at least to assume that he would have been as careful with other sources as well.

Luke's sources for Acts are less easy to identify. However, the "We-sections" (Acts 16:10-17; 20:5-15; 21:1-18; 27:1–28:16)[3] seem to indicate that, at least for these parts of his narrative, the author was using his own

---

[3]The so-called "We-sections" in Acts are those sections where the narrative abruptly shifts from third person to first, that is, from "he/they" to "we." In the *Mercer Dictionary of the Bible*, see Mitchell G. Reddish, "We-Sections," 954-55, and Frank Stagg, "Apostles, Acts of the," 48-49, esp. 49a.

personal travel diary, having apparently been present at the events recorded. Furthermore, thorough studies of the sailing practices recorded in Acts 27 (and perhaps referred to elsewhere) reveal that the author was amazingly accurate in dealing with such issues. In addition, his geographical references to places and his political references to the names and titles of Roman officials and to the names of Roman provinces and the location of Roman cities show both accurate knowledge and generally extreme care. Furthermore, his precision in referring to legal practices relating to the trials of Paul show the same care. Finally, the author shows an excellent knowledge of Greek and great skill in using the language. While this certainly does not prove his qualities as a historian, it is usually the mark of a careful scholar.[4]

Thus we conclude that while Luke was clearly a skillful theologian, he was an equally skillful historian, at least judged by the standards of his time. It appears, therefore, that his narrative in Acts should also be considered as a primary source for our study, not as a secondary source to be relegated to the bypaths of the contemporary historian's task.

It is imperative to remember, however, that Luke was consciously writing history. He wrote Acts several decades after Paul's death.

> It is evident from his prologue [Luke 1:1-4] that Luke set out with the intention of writing history: so much is implied by his plan "to draw up an orderly account," based not only on eyewitness testimony but also on his personal involvement in the course of events "for some time back"[5]

Luke's purpose in writing Acts was "so that Theophilus . . . might be assured of the trustworthiness of the information about Christian origins."[6]

I believe Luke's historical references can be used with confidence, even while allowing him the possibility allowed to any historian—that he may make an occasional error. Luke is demonstrably "incredibly precise in matters of local color and detail."[7] If he is precise in these matters, it is unlikely he would be any less precise in the other details of his record. We can sum

---

[4]Archibald M. Hunter's *Introducing the New Testament*, 3rd rev. ed. (Philadelphia: Westminster, 1972) provides a good, though brief, study of Luke's qualities as a historian. Perhaps the best treatment of the subject is that of F. F. Bruce, "Luke as a Historian," in *The Acts of the Apostles* (Grand Rapids MI: Eerdmans, 1990). Bruce presents very detailed evidence of Luke's qualities as a historian.

[5]Bruce, *The Acts of the Apostles*, 28.

[6]Bruce, *The Acts of the Apostles*, 28.

[7]Luke T. Johnson, *The Acts of the Apostles*, Sacra Pagina 5 (Collegeville MN: Liturgical Press, 1992) 5.

up the value of Acts as a primary source for our study with the words of F. F. Bruce: "of all the NT writers, Luke is the only one who merits the title 'historian.' 'The first Christian historian' is Martin Dibelius's designation for Luke."[8]

Paul's Epistles. "Epistle" is the technical term for the letters of Paul. Some scholars have sought to distinguish between an epistle and a letter, but such an effort seems to offer no new insight to our study. Before the days of the telephone and other electronic means of communication, letters were the primary means of long-distance communication.

Epistles in the first century AD were usually written on papyrus, although occasionally vellum was used. A standard form or outline of the contents was almost always followed. Epistles generally began by identifying the author with the words "From ____." A little thought makes it clear why this was the first thing written in a letter. Today, we sign our letters at the end, but our letters are folded and the whole sheet is visible as soon as the letter is opened and unfolded. Thus we can immediately know who sent it. Ancient letters were rolled up into a scroll. When the scroll was opened, the first thing seen was the identity of the sender. The entire scroll did not have to be unrolled find out who was writing.

The next feature of an epistle was normally the identification of the recipient(s). This was immediately followed by the author's greetings. Thus the opening words were almost always: "From ____ to ____, greetings. . . ."

After these things, we find the body of the letter. Here we read what the author was writing about. This can range from business to personal items, and frequently included both. Most epistles were much longer than our modern letters. Sending epistles from one place to another was not as simple as our modern postal service makes it. Thus, when people wrote, they took the opportunity to communicate as much as possible.

Finally we come to a short farewell, usually accompanied by a wish for health or good fortune, sent by the author to his reader(s). There may also be an occasional final greeting.[9]

---

[8]Bruce, *The Acts of the Apostles*, 27. See "The First Christian Historian," pp. 14-26 in Martin Dibelius, *The Book of Acts: Form, Style, and Theology*, ed. Kenneth C. Hanson (Philadelphia: Fortress, 2004). See also the discussion of Luke as historian in Martin Dibelius and Werner Georg Kummel, *Paul* (Philadelphia: Westminster Press, 1953) esp. 10-12.

[9]Most good introductions to the New Testament or to Pauline studies discuss epistles and their form. Three helpful discussions are Everett F. Harrison, *Introduction to the New*

One major question about the Pauline epistles is whether or not Paul actually wrote all of them. If he did not, then it might appear that those which are not by him must surely be considered as secondary sources. We know that in the common practice of the time in which Paul lived, disciples frequently wrote letters or essays in the name of their teacher, master, or hero. These are called pseudepigraphs. If this occurred in Paul's case, then only those letters actually by him can be admitted *without question* as primary historical sources for our study.

At this point, we should make ourselves aware of those epistles about which a significant number of New Testament scholars raise serious questions convcerning their authorship. Evidence from those epistles which the overwhelming majority of scholars agree came from Paul can perhaps be given more weight than that from the others, at least until we have examined the evidence and drawn our own conclusions. Those which scholars generally agree should be considered as being Pauline with confidence are Romans, 1 and 2 Corinthians, Galatians, Philippians, Colossians, 1 and 2 Thessalonians, and Philemon. The authorship of Ephesians raises questions that have divided scholars.

First and 2 Timothy and Titus present the strongest case against Pauline authorship. These three letters are often called the "pastoral epistles" because they are addressed to the practical activities of believers. Computer analysis of the language used in them suggests that all three were written by the same person. It is just not clear that this person was Paul. Evidence concerning the origins of the manuscripts raises the possibility that these letters originated after Paul's death. Unfortunately, the brevity of the letters makes reaching a more certain conclusion based on the texts alone unlikely, so final resolution of the debate over whether Paul is the author of the pastoral epistles will have to await discovery and analysis of more archaeological or other extrinsic evidence.[10]

Testament (Grand Rapids MI: Eerdmans, 1964) 240-43; Calvin J. Roetzel, *The Letters of Paul, Conversations in Context*, 2nd ed. (Atlanta: John Knox Press, 1982) 29-39; and Paul Ciholas, "Epistle/Letter," *Mercer Dictionary of the Bible* (Macon GA: Mercer University Press, 1990) 258.

[10]See Jerome D. Quinn and William C. Wacker. *The First and Second Letters to Timothy* (Grand Rapids MI: Eedrmans, 2000) 4. For a more detailed discussion concerning the authorship of 1 and 2 Timothy and Titus see Jerome D. Quinn, *The Letter to Titus: A New Translation with Notes and Commentary and an Introduction to Titus, I and II Timothy, the Pastoral Epistles*, Anchor Bible 35 (New York: Doubleday, 1990) 1-20.

Further complicating the question of authorship is the fact that all of the epistles give evidence of some editing, an idea which should not be thought surprising. Also, since Paul regularly used an *amanuensis*, or secretary, their individual styles and vocabularies account for some differences between the various epistles. One such scribe who clearly identified himself is Tertius, who assisted Paul in writing Romans (Rom. 16:22). Paul also appears to have used his companions in writing the epistles. Timothy is associated with so many of Paul's epistles that we can assume he contributed to their content, in addition to serving as Paul's scribe.

Table 1
Paul's Companions in the Epistles

Epistle	Companions Who Assisted Paul
Romans	Timothy, Lucius, Jason, Sosipater (Rom. 16:21)
1 Corinthians	Sosthenes (1 Cor. 1:1)
2 Corinthians	Timothy (2 Cor. 1:1)
Galations	"all the brothers who are with me" (Gal. 1:2)
Ephesians	No known associates
Philippians	Timothy (Phil. 1:1)
Colossians	Timothy (Col. 1:1)
1 Thessalonians	Timothy (1 Thess. 1:1)
2 Thessalonians	Silvanus and Timothy (2 Thess. 1:1)
1 and 2 Timothy	No known associates
Titus	No known associates
Philemon	Timothy (Philem. 1:1)

I am quite familiar with the issues and arguments regarding the authorship of the epistles. My conclusion is that Paul is at least essentially responsible for all of the epistles that bear his name. They were either written by him (directly, through a scribe, or in concert with someone else), which is plainly the case with most of the epistles associated with his name, or they were at the very least written by someone intimately familiar with Paul's activities and thinking. Fortunately, the few epistles about which there is the most disagreement concerning authorship that fall into this latter category have the least bearing upon the historical reconstruction of Paul's life and are least central to this study.[11]

---

[11]Among the better discussions of the issues of Pauline authorship is that of Donald

Furthermore, in all fairness, we must note that if one or more of the epistles were written by an author other than Paul, before we discard or discount its evidence we must raise the issue of that person's competence as a historian, even as we have done with Luke in relation to the material in Acts. In fact, Jerome Quinn even suggests the possibility that Luke may have been the author or amanuensis of the pastoral epistles.[12] Thus it is possible that evidence from an epistle by someone other than Paul may still be valid for a historical reconstruction of Paul's life and ministry.

Reconciling Acts and the Epistles. Accepting both Luke's Acts and Paul's epistles as primary sources does not resolve the historian's dilemma, because of the difficulty in reconciling the chronological data given in Acts with that of the epistles. In the outline below, I have italicized the visits to Jerusalem recorded in each of these sources, which is where we find the crux of our difficulties.

In the Book of Acts, Luke recorded the following details as the basic outline of Paul's Christian life and ministry.

Conversion (Acts 9:1-9)
Preaching in Damascus (Acts 9:10-25)
First visit to Jerusalem (Acts 9:26-27)
Ministry in Jerusalem, Tarsus, and Antioch (Acts 9:28-30; 11:25-26)
Second visit to Jerusalem, bringing financial relief (Acts 11:29-30; 12:25)
First missionary journey (Acts 13:1-14)
Third visit to Jerusalem to attend the great council (Acts 15:1-29)
Second missionary journey (Acts 15:30–18:21)
Fourth visit to Jerusalem to "greet the church" (Acts 18:22)
Third missionary journey (Acts 18:23–21:14)
Fifth visit to Jerusalem (Acts 21:15-26)
Arrest, imprisonment in Caesarea, journey to Rome, imprisonment in Rome (Acts 21:27–28:31)

Guthrie, *New Testament Introduction*, 4th ed. (Downers Grove IL: Intervarsity Press, 1990) 485, 496-528, 545, 572-77, 588-99, 607-49. Here we find a balanced summary of the various positions and carefully reasoned conclusions.

[12]Quinn, *The Letter to Titus*, 1-20. It is important to note that a highly trusted amanuensis was often allowed great freedom in writing the thoughts of the one whom he served. Thus, for example, if Luke were such, he might have taken Paul's thoughts and expressed them in his own vocabulary and syntax.

To compare with the above summary outline of Luke's material in Acts, we also have the information given by Paul in his epistles. This is not all found in one place, but must be drawn together from a number of scattered references.

Conversion and call (Gal. 1:15-16)

Three-year ministry in Syria and Arabia (Gal. 1:17: "nor did I go up to Jerusalem. . . . ")

Escape from Damascus, fleeing the governor of King Aretas (2 Cor. 11:32-33)

Short visit to Jerusalem (Gal. 1:18-20)

Ministry in Syria and Cilicia (Gal. 1:21-24)

Visit to Jerusalem "after fourteen years" for a major conference (Gal. 2:1-10)

Mission throughout the northeastern Mediterranean, indicated by references in Romans, 1 and 2 Corinthians, and Galatians

Visit to Jerusalem to bring an offering from the churches (Rom. 15:25-32; 1 Cor. 16:1-4)

Luke records five visits to Jerusalem while Paul only lists three. The approaches made by historians to reconciling these sources fall into one of four basic categories.

The first, most common, and most superficial approach is to assume automatically that no problem exists in understanding and reconciling the historical data which these ancient documents provide. Such an approach glibly cuts and pastes the evidence provided by these materials, never questioning whether or not the data from one source really fits into that of the other. Like the fabled Procrustean bed, if the evidence does not fit, this approach simply forces it into place with no further thought or comment.

However, when one examines these sources and begins to consider, for example, exactly how many trips Paul made to Jerusalem, problems arise. A different number of such visits is reported in Acts from that which seems to be reflected in the epistles. This very problem gives rise to the next two approaches which scholars make to the biblical materials dealing with Paul.

The second approach to the analysis and use of the biblical evidence is made by those who assume that the evidence from Paul's epistles, since they were written by Paul, the very person whom we are investigating, must be considered as the primary sources for dealing with his ministry. To these historians, Acts becomes a wholly secondary source. If Acts does not agree with the epistles, they automatically assume that Acts is historically in error and simply reject the evidence found there, ignoring it in any attempted reconstruction of Paul's life and ministry. A variation on this approach is made by those who do not believe that all of the epistles are of equal value for historical research. This draws the conclusion that some letters are to be considered primary, while others are either to be ignored or are at least to be considered as secondary.

A third approach comes from the opposite direction taken by the second. This assumes that since Acts purports to set forth the history of the era, it must be primary. Historians here assume that Paul's letters, being written as letters and not as history, are to be treated as secondary sources even though they were written by the very person with whom we are primarily concerned in our investigation. Here the assumption is made that people writing letters cannot necessarily be expected to be accurate in historical references and certainly cannot be depended upon to give all of the data which a modern historian might desire.

A fourth approach, and the one taken here, is to face the fact that there are obvious problems in trying to reconcile the evidence found in the letters and Acts. However, as we have seen, Luke shows every indication of being a careful historian and even a participant in many of the events recorded in Acts. On the other hand, we must assume that since Paul lived through his own ministry, he knew what he was talking about when he referred to events in it. Which one is correct? Can both be?

The fourth approach recognizes that authors are quite selective in the events they record. They are almost always trying to tell their particular part of the story and therefore usually record only those events that lead up to their ultimate message. To illustrate this process, consider the events recorded in Exodus 2:1-10. There we immediately are given the impression that Moses was the first child of his parents. Yet those very verses reveal that he had an older sister and two chapters later we discover he had an older brother. The point is that the birth of Miriam and Aaron were not important to the message the author was communicating in chapter 2. The same kind of thing can be demonstrated over and over again, both in the Old Testament and the New Testament. Thus a difference in the *number* of Paul's Jerusalem visits listed really gives us no problem. Where we run into difficulty is in trying to identify and correlate the visits with one another.

Possibly—perhaps probably—the first visits of both Acts and Galatians are to be identified with each other. If so, then that visit is dated three years after Paul's conversion. However, three years may be approximately thirty-six months or possibly as little as slightly more than twelve months, depending upon whether Paul was using the Jewish or the Roman system of counting the passage of time in giving this reference. Frequently any part of a year was counted as a whole year when chronological references were being made, just as any part of a day might be counted as one day.

Furthermore, the fifth visit of Acts and the visit to bring an offering recorded in the epistles are also probably to be identified. Admittedly, this may not solve all of the difficulties, for in Acts no reference is made to the delivery of such an offering when Paul made his final visit to the church in Jerusalem. Again, that may have been simply an omission by Luke because it was not significant for the story he was recording and the emphasis he was making.

Next, the visit "after fourteen years" may be identified with the relief visit of Acts (the second visit) or with the Jerusalem Council (the third visit). A case can be made for either. Further, there is a problem as to whether or not the "fourteen years" refers to the period following the first visit or to the entire block of time following Paul's conversion. Again, a case can be made for either here as well. For reasons I will give later, I identify Paul's second visit listed in the epistles with the third one listed by Luke. I further conclude that the "fourteen years" reference included the first "three years," thus it goes back to his conversion. Admittedly, these choices will not solve all of the problems of chronology, but they appear to me to be a better choice than any of the other options open to us. Neither Paul nor Luke were trying to write a diary of all of the apostle's activities.

This suggests that using either Acts or the epistles alone as a primary source of knowledge for Paul's ministry is not as simple as it may seem. As Martin Hengel points out,

> In reality, it is only because of . . . [the epistles] that we can assess . . . [the historical reliability] of Acts, while they in turn can only be understood in their particular historical and chronological context as a result of Luke's account. . . . without the account written by Luke, incomplete, fragmentary and misleading though it may be, we would not only find it almost impossible to put Paul and his work in a chronological and geographical setting, we would still be largely in the dark about the development of Paul's great mission around the Aegean and the events that led up to it, and about his concern to go to Rome and to Spain (Rom. 15:22-29). We only realize the significance of Luke's Acts as a historical source if we make a consistent attempt to eliminate the information it contains from our knowledge of earliest Christianity. . . .

Luke's contributions to the historical understanding of Paul is essentially greater than many scholars want to suppose today.[13]

Extrabiblical Sources

When we look for evidence in material outside the New Testament,[14] we are faced with two almost contradictory facts. First, in comparison with other such ancient eras, we possess a large amount of evidence from primary sources relating to the general era of our study. Second, in considering this material we soon discover, however, that we have very little that relates to any particular subject or specific issue about which we are investigating. This leaves us with large gaps in our knowledge about which we can only give educated or partially informed guesses. We also have other areas where we do have quite interesting data but not as much or as clearly presented as we might wish. Consider the following types of sources.

Archaeological sources. Most of the cities in which Paul ministered have been excavated to some degree and some have been almost wholly uncovered. We can actually see buildings which were standing when Paul visited those places. In a very real sense, we can, if we wish, actually walk in his footsteps. From examining these sites and the artifacts which have been found in them, we can at least partially reconstruct daily life as it was in those places when the great missionary served there.

In addition, surface exploration of the regions through which Paul and his companions traveled help us understand the geographical and climatic features that would have influenced those journeys. Further, the recently developed science of undersea archaeology also gives us important insights into the nautical life of those times. This is especially important when we remember how often Paul made journeys by sea rather than by land. We can

---

[13]Martin Hengel, *Acts and the History of Earliest Christianity*, trans. John Bowden (London: SCM Press, 1979). Furthermore, Bastiaan Van Elden, "Some Archaeological Observations on Paul's First Missionary Journey," *Apostolic History and the Gospel: Biblical and Historical Essays Presented to F. F. Bruce on his 60th Birthday*, ed. W. Ward Gasque and Ralph P. Martin (London: Paternoster Press, 1970) 161, points out quite clearly that recognizing Luke as a theologian does not negate him as a historian. He concludes his argument by saying, "I see no incompatibility between theology and history: in fact . . . within the Jewish and Christian tradition . . . [one] cannot be a good theologian unless he is a good historian."

[14]I also discuss these sources in my *A History of the New Testament and Its Times* (Nashville: Broadman Press, 1991).

examine the remains of the very kinds of ships upon which he sailed, some of which also suffered shipwreck.

Yet all of the results of archaeological investigation at best only give us illustrations which we can apply toward gaining an understanding of the environments and conditions under which Paul served. From this kind of investigation, we seldom get the kinds of hard data historians would like to have. Such "hard data" must come from written material.

Jewish sources. A number of ancient Jewish sources exist that help us to understand something of the Jewish background for the New Testament era. Perhaps the most significant for the study of the historical background of those times are the works of Flavius Josephus. Born about AD 37/38, he was trained as a rabbi and gained significant respect for his scholarship, even in Rome. He was a Pharisee and served as a Jewish general in the First Jewish Revolt which began in AD 66. Captured by the Romans, he eventually settled in their capital city. From there he wrote numerous works recounting Jewish history up to the time of that conflict, along with others seeking to make the religion of Judaism both understandable and acceptable to the people of Rome.

The works of Josephus must be handled with care, however, for he clearly wrote with an apologetic purpose. He was viewed as a traitor by his own people and with some degree of suspicion by his Roman audience. Thus his writings are demonstrably self-serving. Throughout he was trying to defend his own record. At the same time, his writings cannot be ignored, for in many instances, despite their problems, they are the best source we have for the study of the history of the era.

Two other Jewish sources, *1 and 2 Maccabees*, are found in the Apocrypha of the Old Testament. While these clearly end long before the time we are studying, they help us understand some of the issues related to the Judaizers, the Hellenists, and the Pharisaic-Sadducaic controversy, with all of which Paul had to contend in his ministry.

The Dead Sea Scrolls from Qumran and the related Damascus Document also give some limited help in understanding the era. While the significance of these is generally limited to the region of Palestine, they still add some depth to our understanding of the times, places, and thought forms that may have influenced Paul and with which he had to deal.[15]

---

[15]The work of Jerome Murphy-O'Conner, *Paul and Qumran* (London: Geoffrey Chapman, 1968) is especially helpful here.

Last among the Jewish sources we must consider in this era is that collection known by the generic term of "rabbinic literature." While we must acknowledge that it was not even completed, much less codified, until long after Paul's death, parts of this body of literature must at least be considered in our study. It is of particular value as it reveals the ways in which rabbis were trained to think and to interpret Scripture. Paul was so trained, and this material clearly illustrates the kind of thinking he did both in his sermons and in his epistles.

Christian sources. The only Christian materials, other than the writings of the New Testament, which can at all possibly be called primary sources for the study of this era are those designated as the writings of the church fathers. These were Christian writers who supposedly had actually known the apostles and their companions or who were involved with others who had. Their writings extend from the final days of the writing of the New Testament to the last half of the second century.

Among these are *1 Clement*, written by a member of the church of Rome. Clement's writings give us information that aids our understanding of early postapostolic Christianity and the influence Paul had upon it. Also from this period is the *Didache*, often called by its anglicized title, *The Teaching of the Twelve Apostles*. The *Didache* sets forth a summary of early church polity and discipline. It is of particular value in understanding some of Paul's epistles. The *Didache* has been variously dated from as early as AD 60 to as late as AD 150.

Remarkably similar is the *Epistle of Barnabas*, which comes from about the same era. Although unlikely to have actually been written by the Barnabas of the New Testament, this letter seeks to point out that Judaism was not God's final word but a preparation for his ultimate revelation in Jesus Christ. All of these sources help us understand the developing churches that Paul established, as well as the faith of those other churches that were built upon the foundation of Paul's thinking and preaching.

Greek and Roman sources. The works of five Greek historians must be considered as primary sources for anyone dealing with the history of this era. The first of these is Strabo, whose works were quoted by Josephus. Although he wrote forty-seven books of history, they have all been lost except for quotations found in other sources. He also wrote seventeen books on geography, most of which survive. Here we find extensive help in understanding the physical features of the world of Paul. Two other historians of significance were Polybius and Didorus, both of whom died well before the birth of Christ. Their works are of value primarily as they help us understand the nature of the world in the lifetime of Paul.

Plutarch lived and wrote during the end of the first century and the beginning of the second century AD. He wrote a series of brief biographies about those who built and shaped Rome's greatness. Here we come face to face with the forces which formed the larger world in which Paul ministered. The last Greek historian for our consideration here is Dio Cassius. He lived about a century after Paul, writing an eighty-volume history of Rome. Only eighteen of those volumes survive. The quality of those that survive makes us wish we had the entire collection of his works.

The Roman historians of the era also add detail to our understanding. Livy and Cicero both wrote of Roman history. Both died prior to the birth of Jesus, but they nevertheless help us understand the background of Paul's world. Seutonius, on the other hand, apparently lived during the actual lifetime of Paul. His work on chronology is helpful for the historian. Of even more importance, however, is his work, *The Lives of the Caesars*. This covered the period from Julius Caesar to Domitian, thus relating directly to the entire era of Paul's life and ministry.

Perhaps the most important Roman writer from this period for our purposes was Tacitus. Living into the early part of the second century AD, he produced two works, the *Annals*, and the *History*. These specifically cover the reigns of the Caesars from Tiberius to Domitian. While Tacitus tended to exaggerate the faults of the empire, he does appear to have been quite accurate in identifying the events of major significance for understanding the history of the era. Further, he makes specific references both to Jews and to Christians, pointing out their importance to the empire.

Postbiblical Sources

Beyond the biblical era itself, or at least beyond those who had some chance of actually knowing the early Christians, we come to others of the church fathers. Polycarp and Ignatius were early Christian martyrs, having served as bishops of Smyrna and Syrian Antioch respectively. Also from the same era comes *The Shepherd of Hermas*. These are all considered to be quite valuable as sources for understanding the situations faced by the churches immediately following, and presumably during, the ministry of Paul.

By the middle of the second century AD, a group of writers arose who are known as the "apologists." Their works were defenses or apologies for the Christian faith. Two of the more significant were Justin Martyr and

Irenaeus. While their works are more philosophical than historical in nature, they do give significant information relating to the actual situations which were faced by the early Christians.

Finally, a significant number of writings were produced by Christians of the late second and third centuries AD. These have come down to us under the title of the New Testament *Apocrypha* and *Psuedepigrapha*. Although they frequently claim to have been written during the first years of the Christian era, those claims are demonstrably false. At the same time, some of the information contained in them appears to have validity and must at least be considered by anyone studying the Pauline era.

Modern Interpreters

As noted earlier in this chapter, no one should seek to deal with the issues related to the life and ministry of Paul without first becoming familiar with the major works that have already dealt with this subject. Three works which are available for the study of the chronology and the historical reconstruction of Paul's life are of most help. The oldest is Jack Finegan's *A Handbook of Biblical Chronology*. While quite terse, it brings the best of archaeological and historical investigation to bear upon the subject. Two more-recent studies are Robert Jewett's, *A Chronology of Paul's Life* and Gerd Luedemann's, *Paul, Apostle to the Gentiles: Studies in Chronology*.

Beyond these, a number of other major works exist that seek to help us as we come to grips with understanding Paul the man, the minister, the missionary, and the theologian. No listing of books in this category will be wholly satisfactory to any other interpreter. However, one has stood out for me as more helpful in getting to know Paul as a man than any of the others: Reginald E. O. White's *Apostle Extraordinary*. Several more-recent works are also quite useful, for example, C. J. den Heyer's *Paul: A Man of Two Worlds*; Calvin J. Roetzel's *Paul: The Man and the Myth*; and A. N. Wilson's *Paul: The Mind of the Apostle*. Jerome Murphy-O'Connor's *Paul: His Story* provides an especially practical and readable—if at times controversial—narrative of Paul's life. It is based on Murphy-O'Connor's longer and more scholarly, *Paul: A Critical Life*.

Finally, the best help I have found in getting to understand the background of the entire era has been the revision of Emil Schürer's three-volume work, *The History of the Jewish People in the Age of Jesus Christ (175 B.C.–A.D. 135)*. A more-focused treatment of Paul's world is John Dominic Crossan and Jonathan L. Reed, *In Search of Paul*, which is rich in detail about the Roman and Greek context for Paul's ministry. J. Paul

Sampley has also edited a volume of essays under the title, *Paul in the Greco-Roman World*, which provides extensive information on specific topics concerning the world in which Paul lived. One may also find help in my less technical book, *A History of the New Testament and Its Times*.

This collection of books should furnish a good foundation for carrying your study of the life and ministry of Paul further. However, rest assured that all of these references only serve to undergird and add understanding to the biblical texts themselves.

Chapter 2

The Historical Background

Historians generally write using neatly organized outlines. Furthermore, each segment of that outline normally is usually carefully separated from the ones which precede and follow it. Such an approach makes writing easier. It also makes studying the material easier for the reader. Unfortunately, history seldom occurs so neatly compartmentalized. Very infrequently does any one day or year mark a real division between other days and years. Furthermore, almost never does any one single event clearly create a new historical era, at least not in such a manner that it is so recognized by those living at that time.

To the contrary, each new development in history is related to other events around it very much like the strands of a spider's web, being connected with multiple strands to what has gone before and to what follows. Therefore the only way we can ever come close to understanding any single point in the web of history is by attempting to understand as much as possible of what both preceded and followed it, as well as that which surrounds it.

However, the more carefully this is attempted, the more complex the process becomes. Sooner or later we are forced to recognize that we simply do not, nor can we ever, know everything which might have influenced a specific historical event. It might depend upon something so vast as the movement of armies across continents or something so nondescript as a migraine headache or a bout of malaria on the part of a soldier on guard duty, or an upset stomach on the part of a theologian (or historian).

In attempting to set the stage for our understanding of the life and ministry of Paul, we will seek to bring together a brief description of what appears to have been the major historical influences that acted upon him and his world, both directly and indirectly. These clearly involve the major events of world history which enveloped his life. They just as clearly involve the major thought patterns which bore upon and helped shape the mental processes of the apostle from Tarsus, as well as those of his contemporaries. To these we now turn our attention.

The Times

Paul's ministry seems to have occurred during the years from about AD 30 to about AD 64.[1] However, since he grew up in Tarsus during the period prior to these dates we need to be concerned, as a minimum, with the whole period from the beginning of the first century AD to the date of his death. The entire era with which we are concerned was one of great turbulence for the northeastern part of the Mediterranean world. Few things could be looked upon as certain in those days.

At the center of the Roman Empire, a variety of rulers with extremely varying capabilities controlled Rome. The first of these was Augustus (27 BCE–AD 14).[2] A generally enlightened ruler, Augustus sought to maintain peaceable conditions in his empire so that tax money flowed into Rome from all over the empire in an unbroken stream. Disturbed by the obvious failure of the reign of Archelaus, a son of Herod the Great and governor (ethnarch) of Judea and Samaria, Augustus established Judea and Samaria as a third-class Roman province, governed by procurators appointed by the emperor. In an attempt to prevent corruption of the procurators, their terms of service were limited by the emperor to a period of three years.

This rapid turnover of governors in the land of Judea meant that no governor ever really had time to learn how to govern the region from experience, thus producing constant turmoil in that province. This in turn bred conflict within the Jewish parties of the region as they sought to establish and maintain their own political power with each new governor. Outside the region of Palestine, however, a general period of stability was enjoyed in those other areas of the northeastern Mediterranean with which we are concerned.

---

[1]Additional material for understanding this period can be found in my *A History of Bible Lands in the Interbiblical Period* and in my *A History of the New Testament and Its Times*. Further help may be found in John Dominic Crossan and Jonathan L. Reed, *In Search of Paul* (New York: HarperSanFrancisco, 2004) and in Floyd V. Filson, *A New Testament History* (London: SCM Press, 1965) 3-33, 134.

[2]Helmut Koester, *History, Culture, and Religion in the Hellenistic Age*, vol. 1 of *Introduction to the New Testament* (Philadelphia: Fortress Press; Berlin: Walter de Gruyter, 1982) 301-307.

Table 2
Roman Emperors

Emperor	Dates of Reign
Augustus	27 BCE–AD 14
Tiberius	AD 14-37
Caligula	AD 37-41
Claudius	AD 41-54
Nero	AD 54-68

Tiberius (AD 14-37) succeeded to the throne of Rome following the death of Augustus, his adopted father.[3] No official process of succession had been established in Rome, but Augustus's adoption of Tiberius as both son and successor solved the immediate crisis, though a brief period of tension was felt in Rome itself.

Especially concerned with conditions throughout the empire, the new ruler sought to curb burgeoning governmental expenses and adopted an official policy of financial austerity which was imposed upon governmental administrators. Tiberius also sought to insure governmental stability in the provinces by providing for more lengthy terms of service for his appointees. This was of special benefit to the regions of Palestine. While Tiberius's economic and administrative policies brought him popularity throughout the empire, they aroused intense dissatisfaction among the bureaucrats in Rome.

The emperor Tiberius unwisely left much administrative responsibility in the hands of the prefect of his imperial guard, Sejanus. Sejanus sought to consolidate his power by bringing numerous charges of treason against those nobles who might be rivals to his own power. However, the bitter fruit of this was that Tiberius ultimately became suspicious of Sejanus's own loyalty. The prefect was arrested and executed in AD 31 as an outgrowth of his anti-Semitic policies which Tiberius assumed were undercutting his own policies.

This act on the part of Tiberius catapulted the Jewish people into the center of the empire's consciousness and established them as a people who

[3]Koester, *History, Culture, and Religion in the Hellenistic Age*, 306-308. (For an illustration of the so-called Julio-Claudian House, Octavius to Nero, see the "family tree" in Koester, p. 309.)

had the good will of Caesar. On the other hand, Tiberius's fears of anything that might smack of treason meant that anyone who might be suspected of disrupting the peace of the empire, or even of not preserving it adequately, was forced to beware of Tiberius's wrath.

Upon the death of Tiberius, and according to Tiberius's wishes, Caligula (AD 37-41) was named emperor.[4] Orphaned at the age of seven by the probable assassination of his father, Caligula had been raised by his mother and two other elderly women. These experiences would probably have given to him a distinctly warped personality, even if he had not had congenital mental problems (as many historians believe). A serious illness shortly after his accession as emperor clearly added to his mental aberrations.

Following that illness, Caligula sought to demonstrate his absolute authority and his disdain for anyone else by having his horse named a Roman Senator and himself declared a god. He also reversed his predecessor's policies regarding anti-Semitism. An irrational and capricious ruler, his instability made the entire empire unstable. Such a state of affairs ultimately led to his assassination by his own Praetorian Guard in AD 41.

Up to this time, the emperor had always been named by the Roman Senate, even though they had normally acceded to the request of the ruling Caesar. However, in the years we have been considering, the army's power had been steadily growing. Upon the death of Caligula, the army forced the Senate to name one of their own, Claudius (AD 41-54), as the new emperor.[5] Although the manner of Claudius's accession to power revealed an inherent instability in the Roman government, his rule turned out to be surprisingly stable and effective. He had been a petty administrative bureaucrat and turned to others like him for his political appointments. Although he alienated Rome's nobility by appointing freed slaves to major administrative positions, their experience as stewards of their masters' affairs qualified them eminently for their new duties. Thus Claudius restored peace and political stability to the empire during the time when Paul's missionary endeavors were most likely just beginning.

Even though the beginning of the reign of Claudius showed him to be an unlikely prospect for greatness, Claudius rose to the occasion and must be considered to be one of Rome's most able rulers. His rule made the mis-

---

[4]Koester, *History, Culture, and Religion in the Hellenistic Age*, 308-10.

[5]Koester, *History, Culture, and Religion in the Hellenistic Age*, 310-11; Filson, *A New Testament History*, 236; and George Ogg, *The Chronology of the Life of Paul* (London: Epworth Press, 1969) 99-103.

sionary travels of Paul and other Christians much easier than they could have been before his reign and certainly much easier than they were after it.

Although Claudius had a natural son, he was succeeded in imperial power by his adopted heir, a great-nephew by the name of Nero (AD 54-68).[6] Shortly thereafter, Claudius's natural son died, most likely as the result of poisoning at the instigation of Nero. This set the stage for what was to become one of the more brutal reigns ever experienced by Rome.

Nero began his reign by revealing himself to be a fairly able administrator. However, he was beset by a highly developed ego which was joined with a belief that he was an artist in many fields. To these qualities was added a deep streak of violence. Needing finances, he turned to an ancient law and charged many of Rome's leading citizens with treason. The very fact that they were so charged by the emperor clearly revealed their guilt, so those accused were executed. Under Rome's laws, the property of persons so executed became that of the Caesar. Under this guise of legal murder, Nero was able to continue paying the expenses of his lavish entertainments, entertainments which were designed to gain him popularity with the masses.

Nero apparently had the city of Rome burned in AD 64, so that he could rebuild it in accord with his own artistic tastes. In an attempt to turn the anger of the suddenly homeless people away from him, he blamed the Christians for the fire, giving rise to the first major Roman persecution of the followers of Christ. Nero's policies cost him friends and raised many enemies. When the Praetorian guard finally rose against him, he committed suicide, bringing a violent end to a violent life.

During the reigns of these emperors, Augustus to Nero, the provinces of the empire generally reflected the quality and policies of the ruler in Rome. Political and economic conditions in Judea and Samaria, however, were always far less than ideal. In general, the problems there were accentuated by the weaknesses of the local rulers who were appointed to serve following the death of Herod Agrippa (AD 44). Their failings became steadily more obvious. Unrest and violence coupled with political intrigue and the quest for power became the rule of the day in Jerusalem and Judea. As a remote province on the far edge of the empire, its procurators were gen-

---

[6]Koester, *History, Culture, and Religion in the Hellenistic Age*, 311-14; and Filson, *A New Testament History*, 296-97.

erally much less than Rome's best. Their weaknesses in turn brought out the worst in the Jewish leaders with whom they had to relate in governing. The end result of these declining conditions was the First Jewish Revolt which began in AD 66 and ended with the destruction of Jerusalem in AD 70.

Throughout this period, the fortunes of the Christian community which was rooted in Jerusalem were directly tied in with the conditions faced by the all the other people in the region. Their fate as affected by politics and economics was neither better nor worse than that of those people around them.

With the destruction of Jerusalem and the Jewish state, however, the ongoing conflict between the officials of Judaism and Christianity came to an end, leaving a "total victory for Gentile Christianity about AD 70."[7]

The Thought Patterns

While the actual history of the first century AD clearly affected all the people in the world during Paul's lifetime, our concern with the thought patterns of the day primarily relate to Paul himself, to those among whom he served, and to those with whom he shared his ministry. At this point we are seeking to understand what it was that made Paul think, write, and act as he did. This can only be done as we strive to understand the various strands that were woven together in his mental and intellectual development.

Jewish Thought Patterns. Paul described his own background in terms which both clearly and vividly emphasize that Jewish nature which was fundamental to his basic personality. When he was arrested in Jerusalem, he proclaimed to the people who accused him:

> *I am a Jew*, born at Tarsus in Cilicia, but brought up in *this city* at the feet of Gamaliel, *educated according to the strict manner of the law of our fathers*, being zealous for God as you all are this day. (Acts 22:3, emphasis added)

Later, when on trial before the Sanhedrin, he asserted, "*I am a Pharisee, a son of Pharisees*" (Acts 23:6, emphasis added). Again, on trial before Agrippa, he insisted, "According to the strictest party of our religion, *I have lived as a Pharisee*" (Acts 26:5, emphasis added). And to his friends in Philippi, he described himself as having been "circumcised on the eighth

---

[7]Jacob Jervell, *The Unknown Paul* (Minneapolis: Augsburg Publishing House, 1984) 13.

day, of the people of Israel, of the tribe of Benjamin, *a Hebrew born of Hebrews; as to the law a Pharisee*" (Phil. 3:5, emphasis added).

From these personal descriptions, we may conclude that Paul was indeed a Jew, a Pharisee, and had been specifically trained as a rabbi. These things tell us a great deal about him. Clearly he was proud of his Jewish heritage and would have known it quite well.[8] As both a Pharisee and a rabbi, he would also have been a thorough student of the Hebrew Scriptures and of the rabbinic traditions. He would have believed in the Hebrew Scriptures as the revelation of God which taught the people of Israel how to live a good and godly life. He would also have believed in the Hebrew Scripturew as the *Torah* (Law/Instruction) of God which set forth God's demands upon His people.

As a Pharisee, Paul would have devoted extreme zeal to obeying that Law of God. He knew with great clarity what it meant to be righteous and was a part of a group who were among the most moral people who ever lived. Furthermore, being a Pharisee meant that Paul believed in life after death. This commitment would have clearly separated him from the influential Sadducees of his day.[9]

Furthermore, because of his Jewish heritage, Paul would have had a thorough belief in the sovereign Lordship of the God of Israel. In addition he would also have had a deep commitment to the future hope of his people, particularly as it applied to the coming of God's delivering Messiah.

In addition, by being a part of the Jewish people and of the Judaism of his day, the young rabbi from Tarsus would have been committed to the synagogue as a means of sustaining and propagating his spiritual heritage. These local congregations were later to influence significantly his approach to the spread of the good news about Jesus. He would have had a deep commitment to the corporate relationship that existed among the Hebrews and to the covenant relationship that bound them to their God and to one another. Paul would also have believed that God was the great Redeemer-Deliverer of His people. As a final part of his Jewish heritage, he would have been taught to believe that of all the peoples of the earth, Israel alone was chosen for a special relationship with God.

---

[8]The Judaism of Paul's day is thoroughly and perhaps best described in Koester, *History, Culture, and Religion, in the Hellenistic Age*, 205-80.

[9]For more information about the Pharisees and their impact on Paul see C. J. den Heyer, *Paul: A Man of Two Worlds*, trans. John Bowden (Harrisburg PA: Trinity Press International, 2000) 35-38.

Greek Thought Patterns. Paul, however, was more than a Jew and his world was far larger than Jerusalem and its environs. He had proudly spoken Greek to the Roman tribune who had arrested him in Jerusalem, saying, "I am a Jew, from Tarsus in Cilicia, *a citizen of no mean city*" (Acts 21:39, emphasis added). His birthplace indicates that in addition to his Jewish heritage he possessed a Greek background as well. This background is seen in the fact that Paul's later writings reveal a significant knowledge of the Greek poets, playwrights, and philosophers. Tarsus was a major center of Greek learning and philosophy. Even though it never attained the stature of Athens, it was no provincial backwater either. In his formative years, Paul was clearly exposed to the intellectual influences of the very best of Greek culture.

The ancient Greeks had emphasized the intellect as the basis for living the good life. Paul was clearly educated in the thoughts and writings of some of those Greek thinkers. He used their materials on occasion with as much reverence as he showed to his own Jewish Scriptures. However, he did show that his approach to philosophy was for the illumination of the mind. He wove the best of the Greek philosophers into his being with the best of the Pharisaic and rabbinic traditions. It seems to have taken the later experience of dealing with the philosophers of Athens to teach him finally that the Gospel he proclaimed was far more than a philosophy. (See the later discussion of his ministry in Athens and its influence upon that which followed in Corinth.)

For most of his ministry, however, Paul was communicating to people who had been brought up in the Greek world of Macedonia and Asia. His knowledge of their way of thinking and of their leading thinkers prepared him to communicate to these people quite effectively. On the other hand, in Paul's day, much of the philosophy of Greece had degenerated into "fancy" thinking rather than being a serious approach to the basic questions regarding the true nature of life which characterized much of the earlier Greek philosophers and writers.

Furthermore, Paul shows a clear acceptance of the Greek commitment to the idea of a sound mind in a sound body. The Greeks brought major athletic contests to the world and Paul shows both a knowledge of and a commitment to their emphases upon physical training and discipline. Such a commitment would have been impossible for a Pharisee of Jerusalem. Being from Tarsus made this commitment both possible and practical for Paul. He certainly found in that emphasis upon physical training a pattern for the overall discipline of Christian living.

Related to but not identical with Greek thought patterns was the Greek language itself. Perhaps the most significant change wrought by the conquest of the eastern Mediterranean world by Alexander the Great was that Greek became the language of international relations, commerce, and communications. By the time of Paul, when one traveled across national borders language presented no significant barrier to communication. *Everyone* spoke Greek. Furthermore, the elegant classical Greek of the ancient philosophers had borne a more useful daughter, *koine* ("common") Greek.[10] This was the language of the common people of the empire. Thus when Paul sought to carry the message of Jesus into "all the world," he could be understood by ordinary people wherever he went.

Roman Thought Patterns. Paul's intellectual and spiritual heritage, however, included even more than just the Jewish and Greek strands. Paul was a Roman citizen as well, and quite proud of it. To the Romans of his day, citizenship was an inestimable treasure (see Acts 22:25-29). Roman citizens had a particular heritage and developed a certain attitude toward life which was clearly revealed in Paul's ministry and writings.

Paul used the nature of Roman citizenship and colonization practices to illustrate the Christian's part in the kingdom of God (see, for example, Eph. 2:19; Phil. 3:20). He also saw Roman citizenship as something to be prized because of the rights and privileges it granted. Furthermore, when Rome conquered new territories, colonies were established in them which were made up of retired soldiers. This led Paul to describe the church in terms of a "colony of heaven" ("our commonwealth is in heaven," Phil. 3:20).

Paul also used his Roman citizenship on more than one occasion as a means for getting himself (and his companions) out of a tight spot. Roman government, whether imperial or provincial, bore a very special responsibility to Roman citizens, and Paul well knew and appreciated that fact.

An additional contribution to Paul's life and ministry that Rome made is not directly a "thought pattern." This was the empire itself. As Rome conquered territories, she opened borders, making it possible for travelers and traders alike to move from one nation to another with no hindrance. Further, Rome built a major system of highways throughout her empire. The basic purpose of these highways was to make it easy for her legions to move

---

[10]The development of *koine* Greek is described in Koester, *History, Culture, and Religion, in the Hellenistic Age,* 101-103.

rapidly around the empire and for dispatches and taxes to flow just as easily
into the coffers of the great city itself. These highways were patrolled by
Roman soldiers to keep them safe. These roads made it easy for Paul, his
companions, and his fellow laborers to move around the empire carrying the
good news of Jesus. It also made it easy for him to send and receive
messages and letters from the churches he had started.

These three roots—the Hebrew, the Greek, and the Roman—helped
shape the message and ministry of Paul. In fact, they made him what he was
and made it possible for his ministry to accomplish what it did. No one can
fully understand or appreciate the life and ministry of the great apostle without taking each of these individually and all of these collectively into full
consideration. We omit any one of them from our thinking at the peril of
failing to understand fully the forces that shaped Paul, his companions, and
his audiences.

The Chronology of Paul's Life and Ministry

Before we can proceed further with our study of the life of Paul, we
must grapple with some fundamental issues related to the chronology of his
life. No such thing as an *approximately* accurate chronology exists. Either
a date for an event is correct or it is not. On the other hand, given the fact
that in Paul's lifetime there were no consistent methods for counting and
recording time, we do not really have the kind of chronological information
regarding his ministry that a modern historian would like to have. Therefore
in most instances we can only arrive at approximate dates for the events of
his life. Some of these can be very well established, almost to the point of
certainty. Others can be established with a high degree of probability. But
many of the dates of Paul's life and ministry are only the educated guesses
of scholars who bring together their knowledge of distances, highway and
sea conditions, climatic influences, and the chronological periods into
which such events must fit.

Paul's entire ministry must clearly be fitted into the period between the
crucifixion, resurrection, and ascension of Jesus on the one hand and the
final imprisonment of Paul in Rome on the other. He obviously cannot have
begun his ministry before the one and the known events of his life do not
continue after the other.

These limits confine us to a very narrow span of ancient history. For
this reason, any reconstruction of the dates of Paul's ministry will not differ
very much from some other reconstruction. The major differences in the
dating of Paul's ministry generally depend upon the presuppositions of the

particular historian doing the dating. However, while reconstructions of the dates of Paul's ministry do not vary significantly from each other, all historians must make an effort to establish these dates for themselves. This then is the next task to which we must address ourselves and one of the primary tasks of this book.

Basic Issues: Absolute or Relative? Until very recent times, most Pauline historians have sought to reconstruct Paul's life with absolute dates, based upon the data given in Acts and/or the epistles as they are connected together with the known, firmly fixed dates of the history of the Roman empire. These approaches first began by assuming that Luke's material in Acts was wholly reliable (from a historian's perspective) and that Paul's occasional references in his epistles could all be fitted into Luke's data. More recently, however, as we have already noted, some have questioned Luke's accuracy as a historian, seeing him primarily as a theologian. These have sought to establish Paul's dates wholly by his epistles and to fit Luke's data into this framework, if possible.

The major problems raised by this approach center upon the actual number of visits Paul made to Jerusalem and the purpose(s) of each. (We will discuss these in greater detail shortly.) But both of these approaches have been controlled by the historians' initial desire to place a specific date upon each event to which reference has been made.

In even more recent times, however, some scholars have sought to ignore the need for absolute dates. This newest approach focuses upon establishing a relative chronology or relationship between the known events of Paul's life. This usually begins with the attempt to arrange Paul's letters in a relative relation to one another, based upon the study of the contents of each. This approach also begins by determining which letters can be proven (assumed?) to have actually been written by him and which were (or may have been) written later by some of his disciples in his name, setting forth his approach to new situations and conditions. Only after the relative arrangement of the epistles is established do these historians even begin to try to fit the historical data of the epistles and Acts into the pattern of Roman history. Finally, it is only after this that specific dates are assigned to any event. Sometimes, no specific chronology will even be suggested by the scholars making this approach, leaving that process to the student rather than being done by the historian.

Weaknesses can be found in any of these approaches. In fact, it is not a matter of which approach to use or which is right. Rather, all such approaches can furnish vital data for the historian to consider. The basic task of the historian is to reconstruct history and to understand what happened. If any of these approaches is ignored, this task cannot be fully accomplished.

Chronological Data from Acts. We concluded in the prior chapter that "the author of Acts was at once historian and theologian."[11] Since he was a historian, the Book of Acts abounds with chronological data of various kinds. First, there are references to historical events or people who are found and can be identified in the secular world. Among these are Roman rulers or people in authority, such as Annas and Caiaphas (Acts 4:6), King Herod (Agrippa I) (Acts 12:1, 20-23), Sergius Paulus, proconsul of Cyprus (Acts 13:7), the emperor Claudius (Acts 18:2), Gallio, proconsul of Achaia (Acts 18:12), Felix and Festus, governors of Palestine housed at Caesarea (Acts 23:26; 25:1), and King Agrippa (Acts 25:13). These references all give a careful historian an opportunity to relate the events found in the biblical narrative where these names appear with ancient secular records.

The second kind of chronological data given in Acts is references to events or seasons that occurred annually or periodically. These sometimes provide information concerning the season of the year with which we are dealing in considering specific events. Such data relate to the Jewish festivals, such as Pentecost or Passover. They also relate to the time of year when certain things normally happen, such as the appropriate time for sailing in the northeastern Mediterranean (Acts 27:9).

The third kind of historical data found in Acts relates to the number and sequence of events. Thus Paul (1) started to Damascus, (2) was converted, (3) stayed some time, (4) fled to Jerusalem, (5) stayed there for a period, and then (6) fled to Tarsus (Acts 9:1-6, 23-30). Similar to this is the record of Paul's three missionary journeys, followed by his final trip to Rome as a prisoner facing judgment. These kinds of data allow us to put events in their proper relationship to one another.

The historical data found in Acts is only to be expected, for the book purports to be a history of the spread of Christianity from Jerusalem to Rome. At the same time, we need to realize that Luke had to be quite selective in the events he recorded. He obviously left out many things that occurred and about which he knew but which were not relevant to the story he told. Thus, merely because something is not mentioned in Acts does not mean it did not occur. Such things were simply not a part of the chain of

---

[11]Robert Jewett, *Dating Paul's Life* (London: SCM Press, 1979) 8.

events that Luke was following. This kind of selectivity is practiced by anyone writing history.

Chronological Data from the Epistles. The chronological references in the Pauline epistles are of the same kind as those found in Acts, but are much more difficult to locate and to interpret. As we have noted several times, Paul was writing letters, not recording history. He occasionally reported historical events, but in most instances was in no way trying to present a narrative report of what had happened to him. In one place he gave a summary of some of the things that had befallen him, but a brief consideration will reveal that we simply do not possess enough detail here to be able to reconstruct any specific series of events from the report. Consider:

> Five times I have received at the hands of the Jews the forty lashes less one. Three times I have been beaten with rods; once I was stoned. Three times I have been shipwrecked; a night and a day I have been adrift at sea; on frequent journeys, in danger from rivers, danger from robbers, danger from my own people, danger from Gentiles, danger in the city, danger in the wilderness, danger at sea, danger from false brethren; in toil and hardship, through many a sleepless night, in hunger and thirst, often without food, in cold and exposure.
>
> (2 Cor. 11:24-27)

Many of these "events" are mentioned neither in Acts nor anywhere in the other epistles. Thus we have no way by which any of these events can be placed precisely into Paul's life and ministry. At the same time, there is no question but that they happened to him and were a part of his ministry. Paul did not just invent the list.

In addition, Paul gave some specific chronological data in his epistles which must be considered. He wrote of a period of time spent in Arabia where he apparently sought to understand what had happened to him in the experience of conversion. He then told, in quite specific terms, of two visits to Jerusalem:

> After *three years* I went up to Jerusalem to visit Cephas, remained with him *fifteen days*. . . . Then after *fourteen years* I went up again to Jerusalem with Barnabas. (Gal. 1:18; 2:1, emphasis added)

These references, though given with a certain precision, are subject to some degree of interpretation. For example, "three years" can actually be three full years or one year and parts of two others, depending upon the system of reckoning which Paul may have been using.[12]

Paul also occasionally gave indirect historical references, as when he wrote: "At Damascus, the governor under King Aretas guarded the city of Damascus in order to seize me" (2 Cor. 11:32). Such references furnish us with additional data by which to reconstruct the ministry of the great apostle. According to this statement, Paul's time at Damascus has to have been during the time of a ruler named Aretas. Furthermore, it would appear that this also had to be at a time when Rome's control was weak enough in this region for a local king to seize power.

Finally, chronological references can be found in quite incidental citations. Paul wrote at one place of being with people in Rome ("those of Caesar's household," Phil. 4:22). In other places he speaks of being a prisoner of the Lord. While not specifically being chronological references as such, these do tie the time of writing down to rather limited periods in his lifetime.

Relative Arrangement of the Epistles. An important addition to the chronological data found in the New Testament as it relates to Paul's life may be found in the relative arrangement of his epistles. Robert Jewett has pointed out that

> One of the important unfinished tasks in NT research is to develop a reliable system for dating the Pauline letters. But this is impossible until the major events of his life and ministry are firmly dated to provide a framework upon which to reckon the dates of the individual letters. NT scholars have long searched for "absolute dates" from which the rest of the events could be reckoned. The odd thing about this research is that although such dates can be fairly well established, they cannot be [have not been (?)] made to fit smoothly into any generally accepted outline of Paul's life. The consequence has been an endless process of date juggling.[13]

Furthermore, while arranging the epistles in a relative order is much less precise than other data, given the personal, theological, and organizational references found in the epistles, scholars have generally agreed on the order in which most of the epistles seem to have been written. Clearly, while this may sometimes result in circular reasoning, it frequently can give

---

[12]See Jack Finegan, *A Handbook of Biblical Chronology* (Princeton NJ: Princeton University Press, 1964).

[13]Jewett, *Dating Paul's Life*, 1.

aid in reconstructing something of the ministry of the great apostle. The process of arranging and dating the epistles is the task of an introduction to the New Testament. However, it appears that the following is the most likely sequence.

Table 3
Probable Order of the Writing of Paul's Epistles

Epistle	Where/When Written
1 Thessalonians	From Corinth; probably the first of Paul's letters and the first N.T. writing
2 Thessalonians	From Corinth, soon after the 1 Thessalonians
Galatians	After the Jerusalem Council, or perhaps during the third missionary journey
1 Corinthians	From Ephesus, but two or three years earlier than Romans
2 Corinthians	From Macedonia, sometime after 1 Corinthians and an unknown, harsh letter
Romans	At the height of his career, between AD 54 and 58, from Corinth, as he prepared to go to Jerusalem
Ephesians	From prison, probably in Rome
Philippians	From prison, probably in Rome, but possibly earlier
Colossians	From prison in Rome at the same time as Ephesians and Philemon
Philemon	From prison in Rome
1, 2 Timothy	May be non-Pauline, but certainly possess a core of Pauline material with additions and reediting from late in the first century. The Pauline material is late, either from Rome, or, if Paul was in fact released from his first Roman imprisonment, then sometime thereafter.
Titus	Same as 1 and 2 Timothy

Studying the epistles in this order seems to offer the best hope for understanding Paul's ongoing ministry and developing theology, as well as for understanding the growing structures that were being developed and utilized by the early churches in carrying out their ministries.

Specific Dates. Having established the most likely relative order of Paul's epistles, and having considered the chronological data available from Acts and those epistles, we can now try to establish some specific dates for Paul's life and ministry. There are five fixed points from which we can attempt to develop a chronology of Paul's life by calculating backwards and forwards. The first is Jesus' death. The other four are events mentioned in the New Testament that can be given absolute dates from Roman records.

Jesus' death. It is impossible for Paul's ministry to have begun any earlier than the end of the life of Jesus. Since Paul was an opponent of the early Christians before he became a convert, his ministry could not have begun until some time after the descent of the Spirit on the great Day of Pentecost (Acts 7:57–8:1). Further, it was following Paul's major persecution of the church in Jerusalem that he set out for Damascus, the journey on which he was converted (Acts 9:1-6).

The first problem for us then, is, When did Jesus die? How are we to date the life of Jesus? Again, while the various dates given by historians for Jesus' life cannot and do not vary much from one another, even the slightest variance makes a difference in the period to which we can assign Paul's ministry. The task of assigning dates to the life of Jesus is too involved to be carried out here. Furthermore, it is outside the purpose of this book. The best evidence available at this time appears to indicate that Jesus' crucifixion probably occurred in April AD 32.[14]

This allows us to arrive at the earliest possible beginning point which can be assigned for Paul's ministry. Before it could have begun, we must have had Pentecost (fifty days after Passover), the beginning of the persecution of the church, the internal crisis over the feeding of the Grecian widows, the ministry, arrest, and stoning of Stephen, and then Paul's journey to Damascus (Acts 2:1ff.; 4:1-3; 6:1-6; 6:8-12; 7:54–8:1; 9:1-2).

Herod's death. The death of King Herod (Agrippa I) is reported in Acts 12:20-23. According to Luke's narrative, Paul and Barnabas were in Jerusalem on a relief visit at the time of Herod's death. (Acts 11:29-30; 12:20-23, 25) Chronological material found in Josephus indicates that Herod died in AD 44. This date seems to be as certain as any ancient Roman date.

Therefore this visit of Paul to Jerusalem must apparently be placed no later than Passover of AD 44, for he and Barnabas are said to have been there for that festival and to have returned to Antioch after the death of Herod sometime later in the year (Acts 12:3, 25). This reference therefore appears to give us one firmly fixed point in establishing the chronology of Paul's ministry. (Some historians believe Luke to be wrong here and place

---

[14]To pursue the details that led me to this conclusion, you may wish to refer to my *A History of the New Testament and Its Times*. There I have presented the basic evidence and set forth my reasons for coming to this conclusion.

the Jerusalem visit after Herod's death, thus eliminating this as a fixed point. To me, they do not have sufficient evidence for this conclusion. Unless later evidence forces us to change, we shall assume that Luke is correct here.)

Gallio in Corinth. A third fixed point in Paul's ministry is to be found during his time in Corinth. After eighteen months in Corinth, he was brought before Gallio by the leaders of the synagogue there (Acts 18:11-12). We know that Gallio's term of service as proconsul of Achaia ran from approximately July 1 of one year to approximately June 30 of the following year. We also know that Gallio was in Corinth sometime during the period between "January 25 and August 1, AD 52."[15] The discovery of fragments of a Latin inscription at Delphi established the dates of Gallio's term as proconsul of Achaia as AD 51-52.[16] This means that Gallio was in Corinth from AD mid-51 to mid-52. This data gives us another fixed point with which we must deal. Paul, too, must have been in Corinth sometime from AD mid-51 to AD mid-52.

King Aretas. In 2 Corinthians Paul writes of his escape from Damascus by being "let down in a basket through a window in the wall" (2 Cor. 11:33). The escape was necessary, according to Paul, because "the governor under King Aretas guarded the city of Damascus in order to seize me" (2 Cor. 11:32). Aretas IV held Damascus between AD 37 and AD 39, so Paul's escape must have occurred during these years. Interestingly, this is the only reference to an event to which we can assign a relatively specific date that comes from Paul's writings; the others all are found in Acts.

Felix/Festus. The fifth fixed point in Paul's life that Roman records provide us has to do with the time Felix was replaced by Festus as governor in Caesarea. Paul was in prison there during the time when this transition occurred, and had hearings before both of these men. The date for the transition between these two men can be fixed to the summer of AD 60.[17]

---

[15]Jewett, *Dating Paul's Life*, 39.

[16]Neil Asher Silberman, "The Word of Paul," *Archaeology* (November/December 1996): 30, 34. The precision with which the fragments of the inscription establish Gallio's term may not be quite as precise as Silberman suggests. The inscription places Gallio in Corinth sometime during the period between "January 25 and August 1, AD 52." Robert Jewett, *Dating Paul's Life*, 39. Given the terms procounsels served, this would mean that Gallio was in Corinth *either* from AD mid-51 to mid-52, *or* from AD mid-52 to mid-53. Even so, this inscription gives us a relatively fixed point for dating Paul's presence in Corinth. See Crossan and Reed, *In Search of Paul*, 34.

[17]Koester, *History, Culture and Religion in the Hellenistic Age*, 339-40; and Ogg, *The*

Here we have our last clearly fixed point in Paul's chronology as it relates to known Roman history. Paul could not have sailed for Rome prior to the coming of Festus to Caesarea, but he must have sailed shortly thereafter.

The following table summarizes the likely chronology of, and major events and writing in, Paul's life and ministry.

Table 4
Chronology of Paul's Life and Ministry

AD	Roman Emperor	Paul's Location	Major Events	Paul's Writings
32		Jerusalem	Jesus crucified	
33	Tiberius (14–37)			
34		Jerusalem, Damascus, Arabia	Paul converted	
35				
36		Damascus		
37	Caligula (37–41)	Damascus, Jerusalem Damascus, Tarsus	Met Peter and James	
38				
39				
40		Cilicia		
41	Claudius (41–54)			
42				
43		Antioch of Syria	With Barnabas	
44		Jerusalem (spr.), Antioch of Syria (sum.)		
45		Cyprus	First missionary journey	
46		Antioch of Pisidia, Iconium, Lystra, Derbe		
47		Derbe, Antioch		
48		Jerusalem	Conference	

Chronology of the Life of Paul, 146-70.

49		Troas (fall)	Second missionary journey (spr.)	
50		Philippi, Thessalonica, Beroea, Athens		
51		Corinth		Galatians
52		Corinth, Ephesus & Jerusalem (fall), Antioch (fall)		1 and 2 Thessalonians
53			Third missionary journey (spr.)	
54	Nero (54–68)	Ephesus		
55				1 Corinthians
56		Ephesus, brief journey to Corinth (win./spr.)		2 Corinthians
57		Troas (win.), Macedonia (spr.), Corinth (fall)		
58		Corinth, Philippi (spr.), Caesarea (spr.) Jerusalem (sum.)	Paul arrested and imprisoned	Romans
59		Caesarea		
60		Malta (Nov.)	Paul imprisoned; hearing before Festus & Agrippa II (sum.); sailed for Rome (Sept.); shipwrecked on Malta (Nov.)	
61		Rome	Paul under house arrest	Philemon, Philippians, Colossians
62				Ephesians, 1 Timothy
63		Spain (spr.)?, Crete?, Nicopolis (fall)?		Titus
64		Philippi?, Rome?	Rome burned; imprisonment and death (sum.)?	2 Timothy

Given the information and the data we have surveyed here, we are now ready to turn to the actual study itself. As we attempt to reconstruct and to understand the life and ministry of this extraordinary apostle, we shall draw upon this background and data. Where it is of major significance, we shall consider it in more detail.

Chapter 3

Paul's Earliest Days up to the Missionary Enterprise

Most of us who deal with the life of Paul, either as a matter of history or as a matter of faith and proclamation, have a great deal of difficulty with the early years. Two major periods of silence exist in our knowledge of this period. The first period covers the years of his childhood and those of his education prior to his abrupt appearance in the events surrounding the stoning of Stephen (Acts 7:58–8:1). The second time of silence in Paul's life is that period that began some time after his conversion, between the time of his journey from Jerusalem to Tarsus and when Barnabas brought him to Antioch to help with the mission to the church there (Acts 9:30; 11:25-26).

Admittedly, neither Acts nor the epistles give us any specific or obvious references to events in Paul's life during either of these periods. However, like good detectives carrying out a thorough investigation, we do find a number of clues carefully left behind for our consideration. These indirect references may provide some significant insights into those so-called "silent years." In seeking both to reconstruct the life of Paul and to understand what made him the kind of man he was, we need to consider these silent years as well as those about which we have more specific records, all of which preceded his career as the missionary extraordinary. This was clearly a time of preparation for Paul, and it is to this time we now turn our attention.

Personal Heritage

Paul is introduced to us in Acts as "Saul" (Acts 7:58).[1] It was quite common for Jews of that day who grew up in Roman regions to have dual names, one Roman, the other Jewish. This was especially common when that person had mixed parentage. Quite likely Paul's name was originally the combination *Saulus Paulus*, or vice versa, *Paulus Saulus*. When, in Acts, he first appears in the city of Jerusalem, he was using his Jewish name, since he was at the very least an agent for the Sanhedrin. He may even have been a member of that august body. In any case, much later in his life when his Christian mission took him into Gentile regions, he apparently

---

[1]Although Luke refers to Paul by his Jewish name of Saul until the missionary enterprise on Cyprus, it seems less confusing to refer to him as Paul throughout this study.

started using his Roman name, so that he would not find possible doors of ministry closed to him, because of his hearers' anti-Semitic prejudices.

Tarsus. Paul at one point described his hometown, Tarsus, as being "no mean city" (Acts 21:39). That evaluation might have been considered boastful by those who did not know it, but it was certainly true. Tarsus was located in the Roman province of Cilicia near the Mediterranean, astride the Cydnus River, and was the major seaport of the region. It was actually about six miles from the coast, with most seagoing ships stopping at the harbor nearer the sea. A second section (suburb?) of the city was located ten miles farther north in the rolling hills above the coastal plain.

Tarsus had been established as the capital of the province of Cilicia in 67 BCE. One of its early governors had been Cicero, who set a pattern for those who would follow after him in that position, exercising a very liberal rule, a pattern the citizens clearly came to expect of his successors. Because of the city's strategic location, Tarsus attracted "rulers, enterprising intellectuals, and common laborers. . . . Pompey, Mark Antony, Julius Caesar, Cassius, and even Cleopatra allegedly moored there."[2]

Tarsus was intimately involved in the civil war that began in 49 BCE and for some time stood in danger of being destroyed. However, the city welcomed the victorious Mark Antony in 42 BCE, who reciprocated by making Tarsus a free city, entitled "to govern itself by its own laws, to mint is own coins and to be exempt from export and import duties."[3] Augustus Caesar reaffirmed these privileges after his victory at Actium in 31 BCE, and Tarsus enjoyed the status of being a free city at the time Paul was born.

The city was quite prosperous by the standards of the day, being a center of both agriculture and trade. Tarsus was also quite famous for two major industries, the weaving of linen and the making of tents. This is especially interesting for us, since Paul is later identified as a tentmaker (Acts 18:3). That Paul likely learned such a trade as a youth might be thought to indicate that Paul was of the middle or lower social classes of his city. Not being one of the nobility, it might appear that he had been forced to learn a trade by simple economic necessity as he grew up. However, we need also to realize that he was to become a student of the Jewish Law, the Torah, studying under Gamaliel of Jerusalem. All rabbinic students were

---

[2]Calvin J. Roetzel, *Paul: The Man and the Myth* (Columbia: University of South Carolina Press, 1998) 15.

[3]Roetzel, *Paul: The Man and the Myth*, 15.

required to support themselves by a trade. Thus, becoming a tentmaker may have been simply part of Paul's preparation for his rabbinic studies.

The government of Tarsus at that time established as legal voters all those men who owned property. Within that select group was an even more select group of people who were Roman citizens. These were clearly the aristocracy of the city. Paul was a Roman citizen, having inherited that privileged status from his father. Thus he was certainly a part of the more influential aristocracy of his home city. Perhaps this status into which he was born and in which he grew up prepared him for the ease with which he later addressed governors and kings.[4]

Stoicism. Tarsus was not only famous for its political and economic features, it was also famous for its intellectual achievements, being a major center of stoic philosophy. While not of the status of Athens or Alexandria, both of which drew students from all over the empire, Tarsus did draw a large number of students from the surrounding regions. Further, numerous philosophers from Tarsus went to Rome where they established significant personal reputations. These in turn reflected favorably upon the city from which they had come. At least one philosopher from Tarsus, Athenodorus, became a teacher of the emperor Augustus and from that time on, no Caesar ever had a council of advisors that didn't include at least one philosopher from Tarsus.

Paul may have studied under some of the philosophers of his hometown, or he may simply have been influenced indirectly by their thought and its impact upon his environment. Probably he was not specifically a student of the philosophers so much as being a thinking young man who had been intellectually stimulated by that cosmopolitan environment. His Greek is quite fluent, and possibly came more naturally to him than did the Hebrew/Aramaic of his own people. His later mastery of the audience of philosophers at Athens shows great familiarity with both their ideas and their methods and approaches to dealing with the great issues of life (Acts 17:16-31).[5]

Furthermore, in contrast to Jesus' use of farm and rural illustrations, Paul's speaking and writing are filled with illustrations that indicate he had a city-shaped mind. Paul's allusions refer to the scenes that would have

---

[4]See esp. Martin Hengel, *The Pre-Christian Paul*, trans. John Bowden (London: SCM Press, 1991).

[5]Hengel, *The Pre-Christian Paul*; Martin Hengel, *Jews, Greeks, and Barbarians* (London: SCM Press, 1980).

been familiar to his childhood and adolescence, metaphors of architecture, government, trade, temples, soldiering, and slavery, as well as those of athletic contests, to which we shall return below. Clearly, Paul's home and nurturing in Tarsus helped shape the man he became: serious, thoughtful, confident, accomplished, and hardworking.

Drama and Literature. Like most major Roman or Greek cities of Paul's day, Tarsus had a theater where Greek and Roman dramas were performed. Furthermore, as an intellectual center, the works of the great poets and dramatists of the era were familiar to the well-educated citizens.[6] They were certainly familiar to Paul, as his later references to some of them show. Paul clearly believed that all truth, in whatever form it is found, is God's truth. To the citizens of Rome he later asserted that even without God's revelation to and through the Jewish people, the Romans still had enough of God's truth to have guided them to Himself, leaving them without excuse for not having followed it (Rom. 1:19-23). Such a belief was clearly rooted in his experience in Tarsus of the kinds of knowledge that all educated Romans possessed.

Furthermore, in his later writings to the churches he had established and to whom he had ministered, Paul had no qualms about quoting from the poets and dramatists of his day whenever their words were true. In fact, he quotes them with the same confident assurance that he used when he quoted from the Hebrew Scriptures. We may justly conclude that his background in Tarsus prepared him to communicate effectively and understandably with those of the Roman world who had also experienced those same kinds of influences upon their lives.

Athletic Games. Although not nearly as significant as the Olympic games of Macedonia, Tarsus was the host to a regular cycle of athletic contests known as the Tarsian games. These were a sort of minor olympiad. This emphasis upon sporting contests in the city of Paul's formative years is probably at least one source, if not *the* source of Paul's many later references to such activities. He also likely encountered the biennial Isthmian games while in Corinth. Paul regularly speaks of physical training, of races, of boxing and wrestling matches, and of crowns of victory which were given to winners. He also knew of the oath of honor and the pledge that the rules would be observed which all those who participated in those

---

[6]The subject of the Hellenistic culture with which Paul would have been familiar is treated throughout in Koester, *History, Culture, and Religion in the Hellenistic Age.*

games had to take. The pledge provided: "I will do my best. I will play by the rules. I will compete fairly."

Religion. In the city of Tarsus Paul would also have been exposed to two very different religious influences. First, he himself was a part of the Jewish Diaspora, that segment of Judaism that had been scattered through-out the world following the military crises that had beset their homeland over the centuries. Although those refugees and their descendants were Jewish by birth, by the first century AD the language of these people was almost universally *koine* Greek. This was certainly true in Tarsus. However, this meant that most of them could no longer easily understand their sacred scriptures, which we know as the Old Testament and which were written in Hebrew.

To meet this problem, during the latter part of the era before Christ the Jewish scriptures had been translated into Greek, coming to be known as the Septuagint (abbreviated LXX). Thus Paul's earliest introduction to the faith of his ancestors would have most likely been through the Greek language. Further, in most instances, when he later quoted from the Jewish scriptures in his letters, he quoted from the LXX, probably because this was the version that would have been most readily accessible to those to whom he wrote. Furthermore, if they had been familiar with any version of the Jewish Scriptures, it would have been the LXX.

As a means of holding the Jewish communities together, since they were far away from their homeland and thus removed from any access to the Temple of Jerusalem and its festivals, rituals, and worship, synagogues had arisen in the far-flung cities of the empire, wherever significant num-bers of Jewish people were located. These local synagogues were organized for the purpose of studying their scriptures and for worshipping their God. Paul would certainly have been a part of the synagogue at Tarsus.

The synagogues scattered throughout the empire had given rise to an additional feature of significance for our study. In many of these places, the Jewish congregations had attracted Gentiles to the worship of the God of Israel. Many of these did not actually become Jews, which required ritual baptism and circumcision. These were called "God-fearers" or "devout" persons.[7] Thus Paul was clearly exposed to the "Gentile question" long

---

[7]The subject of "God-fearers" is discussed in detail in Crossan and Reed, *In Search of Paul*, 34-41, 164, 213-14.

before he became a Christian. It was an issue that was certainly discussed in the synagogues and was later hotly debated in the churches.

In Tarsus, however, Paul would also have been exposed to the "Mystery Religions" of the day. While our knowledge of the Mystery Religions is limited, we know that they were deeply concerned with concepts such as lordship, salvation, and eternal life, and that they practiced rites of initiation and ceremonies such as baptism and the Lord's Supper. While these terms became a central part of Paul's later vocabulary, his understanding of them differed widely from that of the Mysteries themselves. The gods of the Mysteries were never "historic" beings. Jesus was. And there apparently was no emphasis upon morality, faith, or love within these pagan religions. Clearly, however, out of his background and exposure to the "mysteries" in Tarsus, Paul was able to draw upon their terminology which would have meaning and thus be more readily understandable to his hearers in later years.

Citizenship. Paul was quite proud of his Roman citizenship which he had inherited from his father (Acts 16:37; 21:39; 22:25). Roman citizenship was a highly prized possession and people throughout the empire who were eligible for it paid significant sums of money to obtain it (Acts 22:28). For Paul to have inherited it marked him out in that area of the world as some-one quite special. We have no way of knowing how Paul's father or some other ancestor obtained his citizenship, but it was not uncommon for Rome to reward faithful soldiers with citizenship upon their retirement, particu-larly if they were settling in a colony in some of Rome's conquered terri-tory. Thus the original recipient of that citizenship may have been a soldier in attendance on or a bureaucrat in the service of one of the governors of Tarsus, perhaps even Cicero.

Given the form of government at Tarsus, having Roman citizenship made Paul a part of the central ruling class and thus a part of the city's aris-tocracy. This meant that from his youth he had access to and was familiar with men of power. In his later life, Paul was always comfortable with such persons, never intimidated by them. That ease of relationship may have its roots deep in his early Tarsus heritage and in his Roman citizenship.

The Jerusalem Background. At some time in his later youth or early adulthood, Paul went (was sent?) to Jerusalem to study for the rabbinate. We know that there he studied under Gamaliel and became a Pharisee (Acts 22:3; 23:6). (Note: he may already have been a Pharisee following in the steps of his father, assuming his father was both a Jew and a Pharisee.) In either case, this would have woven two additional strands into the pattern of Paul's life.

Studying to be a rabbi was an extremely rigorous discipline in the first century AD. Paul would clearly have had to master both Aramaic, the Jewish language of the day among the citizens of Jerusalem, and Hebrew, the language of the Jewish Scriptures. He would also have had to master the content of those Scriptures along with all of the rabbinic oral traditions about them.

Paul's tutor, Gamaliel, even though a Pharisee, was one of the more moderate of the rabbis of his day. This, too, would most certainly have impacted upon the young man's thinking. The discipline of study which was at least developed during this time of his life never left Paul and influenced the demands for disciplined study which he later placed upon all Christians.

On the other hand, being a Pharisee also meant that Paul was one of more strict adherents to Torah, the Jewish Law. The Pharisees' standards of morality and ethics have been unsurpassed over the centuries. What they lacked, a lack which drew the stinging criticism of Jesus, was compassion for and understanding of their fellows. To their credit, they were as uncompromising in their demands upon themselves as they were upon others. This strict legalistic lifestyle also played its part in the later formation of the man who was Paul.

All of these experiences were a part of the heritage out of which Paul grew and which shaped the man who became the church's greatest missionary in the first or any other century. Furthermore, while we have not been able to give any specific details of Paul's youth or childhood, we have been able to sketch a fairly accurate picture of the kinds of things he must have experienced as he grew up in Tarsus and then later was trained in Jerusalem.

Family. We know very little about Paul's family life. While only one of his parents may have been a Jew, it appears more likely with the strength of his Jewish heritage that both were. Clearly, they approved of his studying to be a rabbi. As noted above, he grew up as a Jew in a Gentile city, with deep commitments to the God of Israel and to the Torah of God. He had at least one sister, who also wound up in Jerusalem, apparently having married into one of the more important families there (Acts 23:16). His parents were ambitious for their son, having seen to it that he received the best education and preparation possible for a Jewish youth in a Roman city. As a part of one of the aristocratic families of Tarsus, Paul was prepared by both heritage and family associations for a role of influence and leadership. Long before Paul ever heard of Jesus of Nazareth, Paul was being prepared by the

God of his fathers to be a leader among those who followed and served
Jesus Christ.

Paul's Age. While in Jerusalem for his rabbinic studies, Paul obviously
came to the attention of the leaders of Judaism, including the high priest.
They were apparently attracted both by his orthodoxy and his zeal for
Torah. At least, he was selected by the High Priest and the Sanhedrin to
lead the persecution of the early Christians. He may even have already been
a part of the Sanhedrin himself. At the stoning of Stephen, Paul was present
and was said to have been "consenting to his death" (Acts 8:1). This
expression may only mean that he was simply approving of Stephen's
execution. On the other hand, the Greek word used here could mean that he
was an official part of the Jewish high court (the Sanhedrin) and had
actually voted for Stephen's martyrdom.

If the latter interpretation is true, this has additional implications upon
our knowledge of Paul as a person. To be a member of the Sanhedrin, a man
had to be at least thirty years old and also had to be married. If Paul were
a member of that august body, then we have our only clue to the age of Paul
which is found in the Bible. Further, if he were married, this then gives a
significantly different background for understanding all of Paul's later
concerns with marriage and divorce. If he were married at this point in his
life, the question must be raised as to what later happened to his wife. Did
he leave her behind on his journeys? Had he been divorced or abandoned
by her when he became a Christian, or had she died? These questions are
at the moment unanswerable, but at least they must be given serious
consideration.

Paul's age is another issue. He appears to be quite young and vigorous
at the time we first see him as the leader appointed by the Jewish authorities
in persecuting the Christians. He was also physically active up to the time
of his imprisonment in Rome. The best indication therefore is that he was
probably not much more than thirty at the time of his leading the persecution of the early Christians. If this is so, then his birth must have been some
time around the turn of the era, making him only slightly younger than
Jesus. If, as we have suggested, the crucifixion took place in the spring of
AD 32, then we can assume that Paul would have been about 30-35 years
old at that time. He could hardly have been much younger and was probably
not much older. If he had been significantly older, he would not likely have
been as active as he still was when he went to Rome in the early years of the
AD 60s.

From the Persecution of the Church
to the Damascus Road

To the churches of Galatia, Paul described his early relation to the Christians, writing, "For you have heard of my former life in Judaism, how I persecuted the church of God violently and tried to destroy it" (Gal. 1:13). Other than information given with such broad summaries, little is really known of this era of Paul's life.

Paul first appears in the New Testament under his Jewish name of Saul (Acts 7:58; 8:1). Saul was a name of historic significance among the Hebrews, the name of their first king (1 Sam. 9:17). The name clearly reflects Paul's historic heritage in Judaism: he was of the same tribe as that of King Saul, the tribe of Benjamin. Paul's Hebrew roots went back to the earliest days of their kingdom. This is also reflected in his later self-description as "a Hebrew born of Hebrews" (Phil. 3:5).

While we do not know for certain whether Paul was a member of the Sanhedrin, it is clear he was the Sanhedrin's leader of the official attack upon those early Christians (Acts 8:3; Phil. 3:6). We first meet him in Acts at the stoning of Stephen, as "the witnesses laid down their garments" at his feet (Acts 7:58) and he "was consenting to" Stephen's death (Acts 8:1).

Paul's assault upon the Christians made many of them flee in fear from Jerusalem and its environs. Apparently, they had become so scattered that further attacks upon them in Jerusalem were no longer as fruitful as might have been wished. Thus Paul sought, with the High Priest's approval, to carry the attack farther afield. Damascus was selected as the next center to feel the brunt of his zeal. A large Jewish community in that city was to have served as the base for his new operations in persecution, for Paul carried letters from the High Priest to the synagogues of Damascus authorizing the arrest and return of these "heretics" to Jerusalem where they might be appropriately dealt with (Acts 9:1-2). The reason for this is probably that the Jewish leaders felt that the Roman officials in Jerusalem would be more sympathetic to their cause than those in Damascus, where they had far less influence. Furthermore, Rome's authority in Damascus at that time was actually quite tenuous, for the Nabbatean king, Aretas, was actually in control there shortly after Paul arrived (2 Cor. 11:32).

However, on the way to Damascus, Paul had his conversion experience (Acts 9:3-19). We have no way of knowing what had been going on in Paul's mind during that long journey to Damascus. He could have been thinking about the faith and confidence of Stephen, or that of any of the other unnamed saints whom he had persecuted. Against all odds, the Christians had not only remained faithful in the face of his persecution, they had also continued to grow numerically. Their example certainly gave him much to ponder and also served as seeds that might bear fruit in his own life.

From the Christians' example as well as from their proclamation, along with his own knowledge of the Hebrew Scriptures, Paul's mind had been prepared for his vision of Jesus, the Christians' risen Lord. As both Pharisee and rabbi, he himself had certainly been looking for the Messiah, the hope of Israel.

We have no specific evidence by which to date Paul's conversion. The persecution had begun shortly after the resurrection and ascension of Jesus, which we have concluded to have occurred in AD 32. Some would give the date of Paul's conversion based upon a Christian tradition coming from the second century that Jesus' postresurrection appearances went on for eighteen months, with Paul's vision being the last of these. This would carry us down to the autumn of AD 34. We must acknowledge, however, that such a late tradition must be considered as being of little value as historical evidence.

On the other hand, Paul later said that he had fled from Damascus because of the oppression of the governor appointed by Aretas, the Nabbatean king (2 Cor. 11:32). While historical records of this area and era are quite scanty, the best evidence would indicate that for most of this period, Damascus was under Roman control. The only time when it might have been under Nabbatean control would have been a brief period beginning in AD 37, the time when Caligula became Emperor of Rome. Making these assumptions, we could thus place Paul's flight from Damascus in AD 37 and his conversion apparently three years earlier, in AD 34 (Gal. 1:18). It is at least fascinating that this date also coincides with that of early Christian traditions.

Regardless of when we date Paul's Damascus Road experience, we can readily understand that his name had become one to be feared and despised by the early Christians. Enough time had elapsed for the persecution to have become a frightening, daily reality. No one, either within or without the Christian community, would have imagined that he could ever have become one with those whom he persecuted.

From the Damascus Road to Jerusalem

We need to remind ourselves that we are not, at this point, dealing either with spiritual issues or with those of faith. Our task is that of the historian, not the theologian. Thus our concern here is with events and the man, Paul. Because of this, we are not immediately concerned with the spiritual dimensions or theological implications of what happened to Paul on the way to Damascus. Rather, what we are here concerned with was that Paul's life was at that time and place wholly redirected. Furthermore, from that time and place his thinking had to be (or was) fully reoriented around a totally different center, leaving him with the same set of values for living but a different focal point around which his life revolved. After this event he was never the same again. His energies were channeled into new directions and his old ideas had to be rethought in order to include the new experience which had come into his life.

Following the cataclysmic event which occurred as he journeyed along the highway to Damascus, Paul went on into the city where he was met by a Christian named Ananias. There he was baptized and immediately began telling in the synagogues that he now believed that Jesus was "the Son of God" (Acts 9:20-22). Although the Jews of Damascus had apparently been prepared for Paul's coming, they had not been prepared for anything like this. Further, we can only imagine what the Christians felt or believed at this radical transformation of their former enemy. They had to question and to decide whether this was real or merely a strategy on his part to gain their confidence from which he might later betray them.

Two things stand out in the narrative of what was going on with Paul at this point. First, as soon as he became a Christian, he became what we would call a missionary-evangelist. He sought with vigor to lead others to accept both his new understanding of and his new commitment to Jesus.

Second, Paul also realized that much of his prior understanding of the Jewish faith and hope no longer matched his new experience with Jesus. Many so-called religious people faced with similar situations have opted for denying their own experience and sticking strictly with their traditional orthodoxy. Others have chosen the other direction, wholly rejecting the faith of their fathers in the light of its inability to deal with their present experience.

Paul apparently chose a middle course, deciding that the faith of his fathers had obvious worth, having guided him in the past, while his personal experience could not be denied. Therefore, for a time, he retreated into the

Arabian wilderness to try to think through these things and to make some attempt to reconcile orthodox faith with personal experience (Gal. 1:17). In other words, before rushing headlong into his new life, Paul sought to gain a full, careful, and thoughtful understanding of it.

We have no way of knowing exactly how long Paul spent in the desert of Arabia. Neither do we know how long he had spent witnessing in Damascus before he went into Arabia or how long he remained in Damascus after his return. The entire combination is described as having taken three years, following which he went to Jerusalem (Gal. 1:18). At least one reason for that visit was the apparent desire to make sure that his own understanding of the good news (Gospel) of Jesus was not too far afield from that of the original disciples who were still part of the Jerusalem church.

As we have indicated above, Paul's reference to "three years" does not necessarily have to mean thirty-six months: in the Jewish way of counting time, any part of a year could have been called a year. At the same time, our reconstruction of the time involved makes it appear that this period comes close to being three full years.

What we do know with assurance was that Paul's mission in Damascus had made him obnoxious to the Jewish and secular rulers there. So the Jewish leaders of Damascus "plotted to kill him" (Acts 9:23). They apparently chose as their method the same approach used to kill Jesus. Rather than illegally taking matters into their own hands, they sought to get their dirty work done by the official government under King Aretas of the Nabbateans (2 Cor. 11:32). It would not have been as easy to have accomplished this under the Roman authority of the time, so they apparently seized the opportunity as soon as Aretas became ruler of the region.

Having been warned by a friend of this danger, Paul's disciples sneaked him out of the city under cover of darkness by letting him down over the wall in a basket. By morning, he was well on his way from the city, having escaped the clutches of those who were after him. Once again, he did the unexpected. Instead of fleeing to his home in Tarsus, where he might have been safe, Paul journeyed to Jerusalem, where the Jewish leaders would have been most eager to "get him" and where the Christians would have been most distrustful of his apparent change of heart. No one can ever say that he chose the easy road for mission and ministry.

When Paul arrived in Jerusalem, Luke tells us that "he attempted to join the disciples" (Acts 9:26). Needless to say, they feared him, suspecting that his reported conversion was nothing more than a ruse to get them in his power. The expression used here indicates that he tried repeatedly to join them. His later ministry revealed quite well that he could get along without them, but at this point in time he clearly felt that it was important for him to be identified with the original group of Christians. This record may give some people problems in that Paul himself later recorded of his first Jerusalem visit that he visited with Peter (Cephas) and also saw James, Jesus' brother, but he actually swore an oath that he had seen none of the other apostles (Gal. 1:18-20).

While this offers difficulties, it is also quite possible that, after Barnabas got the church to let Paul in, the other apostles still did not trust him enough to have anything to do with him. The reasons for the fact that Peter and James were willing to spend time with Paul may rest in the fact that Peter was always the bold one, the unofficial leader of the church, and James was growing in importance, as he later became the official leader of the Jerusalem community. At the time Paul wrote Galatians, James was the actual leader of the Jerusalem church, so Paul was showing the Galatians that he had been accepted and had conversed with both the unofficial and the actual church leaders about his message.

Paul's statement that he "remained with Peter fifteen days" may, as some have suggested, refer to the entire length of his stay at Jerusalem. More likely it merely indicates that he spent fifteen days talking specifically with Peter about the details of Jesus' life and teachings.

After Paul had been accepted by the Jerusalem church, he began carrying his message to the "Hellenists" (Acts 9:29). These were the people who were seeking to "modernize" Judaism, making it more acceptable to the Greek and Roman world. While not limited to Jews from the Diaspora, those who were of the Diaspora were frequently of that mind-set. Paul was also of the Diaspora and may have felt an affinity for them. With his native mastery of Greek language and thought patterns, he would certainly have found it easy to communicate with them.

However, Paul was already a wanted man insofar as the Sanhedrin was concerned. His mission to the Hellenists merely raised the level of their hatred directed toward Paul and so another plot was made to kill him. Once again Paul found out about it. This probably indicates that some among the Jewish leaders or their servants had become Christians. It may also have been due to a warning from his old mentor, Gamaliel. At least, from whatever source, Paul was warned of the plot against him, and so his friends hurriedly took him down to Caesarea, Jerusalem's seaport, and shipped him off to his home in Tarsus.

While, as we have noted, some would limit the entire length of Paul's Jerusalem stay to fifteen days, it appears more likely that it was significantly longer than this, extending for at least several months. However, to have journeyed by sea to Tarsus would not have been a likely course for Paul to take during the time of the winter storms which regularly swept the northeastern Mediterranean. Thus he probably made his journey homeward in the early autumn of AD 37.

From the First Jerusalem Visit to the Mission at Antioch

Historians often call the time that extends from Paul's flight from Jerusalem to his later ministry in Antioch of Syria the "silent years." By this is meant that we know nothing of what went on during this time, since Acts gives us absolutely no information relating to the period. However, we must at least raise the question as to whether or not these years were really so silent. The basic issue here is twofold. First, did Paul merely sit in Tarsus, doing nothing but making tents, thinking, and possibly praying until Barnabas finally showed up to bring him to Antioch? Second, if Paul didn't do this, then do we have any indication of what he might have been doing during this time in Tarsus?

The first question must simply be answered on the basis of likelihood. Paul's life up to this time reveals a man who was highly motivated and generally involved in whatever was going on. Furthermore, both Acts and the epistles show that after he became a follower of Jesus, he was busy in both Damascus and Jerusalem preaching about his new faith.

Furthermore, Paul's life after he began his mission with Barnabas in Antioch also reveals the same kind of person. From that time forward he was always busy. He preached, ministered, participated in conferences, and primarily traveled, starting churches all over the northeastern part of the Roman Empire. Given this kind of available evidence, it seems to be highly unlikely that he was not busy doing the same sort of things while he was living in Tarsus. Tarsus was most likely merely a base of operations during that period for some kind of ministry by the man who was to become the missionary extraordinary.

Granting, then, that Paul was probably active in ministry during the years that he made his base in Tarsus, the intervening time can be called the "silent years" only because we do not have any specific record of them. A good detective, however, looks for clues, recognizing that it is seldom likely that absolutely no evidence of activity is left behind. A good historian operates on the same premise. When we begin looking for such clues in our documents, we find them. Paul himself gives us the clues for which we are searching. First, he tells us that during this time he was in "the regions of Syria and Cilicia" (Gal. 1:21). If he had merely stayed in Tarsus, the capital of Cilicia, he would most likely have simply said so, rather than giving the far larger geographical reference of Syria. Furthermore, he later wrote to the Corinthians:

> Five times I have received at the hands of the Jews the forty lashes less one. Three times I have been beaten with rods; once I have been stoned. Three times I have been shipwrecked; a night and a day I have been adrift at sea; on frequent journeys, in danger from rivers, danger from robbers, danger from my own people, danger from Gentiles, danger in the city, danger in the wilderness, danger at sea, danger from false brethren; in toil and hardship, through many a sleepless night, in hunger and thirst, often without food, in cold and exposure.
> (2 Cor. 11:24-27)

Most scholars agree that Paul wrote this material to the Corinthians during his extended ministry at Ephesus on his third missionary journey (Acts 19:8, 10, 22). However, many of the experiences he catalogued here simply cannot be identified with any event of which we know in Paul's life or ministry prior to this. We have no record of his ever receiving thirty-nine lashes. His experience at Philippi is the only recorded occasion of his having been beaten with rods (Acts 16:22). In addition, he mentions "far more imprisonments" (2 Cor. 11:23), yet only one imprisonment can be found in Acts prior to this letter to Corinth, and that too was at Philippi (Acts 16:19-40).

Paul also claimed here three shipwrecks, but not one had been recorded in Acts prior to this point in his ministry. In addition, Paul also recorded an experience of stoning which may be referred to above but which was apparently omitted in Acts (2 Cor. 12:2-4). This is said to have occurred fourteen years earlier. When and where? Any reasonable dating of Paul's ministry clearly places this event in the period when he was supposedly in Tarsus.

The point of all this is that, although Luke leaves us with some "silent years" in the record of Acts, these were clearly not inactive years for Paul. He obviously was busy doing the same sort of things that he did all the rest of his life. He apparently shared the Gospel, started churches, aroused opposition, and suffered persecution.

Thus we must conclude that the years following Paul's return to Tarsus were busy years. They were obviously devoted to his mission. And they were not wholly silent. Paul's own record makes these years speak volumes.

When Barnabas later sought to get Paul to come help at Antioch, he was not seeking out a man whom he merely remembered from a Jerusalem experience some years before. He was seeking out a man who was presently active and whose fame was probably well known in Antioch. After all, Antioch was the capital of Syria, and Paul by his own account had been active in Syria and Cilicia (Gal. 1:21). His reputation had to have been known both to Barnabas and to the congregation at Antioch. "He who once persecuted us is now preaching the faith he once tried to destroy" (Gal. 1:23). The church at Antioch had been started by people who had fled Jerusalem under the assault of Paul's persecution (Acts 11:19-20). They now sought him out to help them grow and develop.

Chapter 4

The First Missionary Journey

During the now not-so-silent years of activity and ministry for Paul in "the regions of Syria and Cilicia" (Gal. 1:21), the Christians who were in Jerusalem and those who had fled from there in the face of the persecution were also being active. Luke summed up this period by writing: "So the church throughout all Judea and Galilee and Samaria had peace and was built up; and walking in the fear of the Lord and in the comfort of the Holy Spirit it was multiplied" (Acts 9:31). Apparently with the conversion or desertion of Paul, depending on which side one was on, the persecution of the Christians had stopped, or at least been dropped for a while.

Some of the reasons for this relaxing of the persecution of the Christians by the Sanhedrin are obvious and others may be deduced from the historical background. The conversion of Paul, whereby the Sanhedrin lost its public leader of the persecution, would have been both a shock and an embarrassment. A period of time was needed for them to make a damage assessment and for the rethinking of their whole approach to those early Christians and to the problem which they had created for the Jewish leaders.

In addition, the obvious fact was that the persecution of the Christians, instead of stopping or even slowing the spread of their faith, had to the contrary seemed to accelerate both their numerical growth and their geographic expansion. True, many persons had fled from Jerusalem and the congregation there was noticeably smaller. But those who had fled had carried their faith with them, sharing it wherever they went (Acts 8:4, 25, 40; 11:1, 19-20). Churches now existed throughout the region.

Affairs in the empire, however, probably had played the most important part in bringing an end, however temporary, to the Christians' persecution. Caligula had become emperor in AD 37, about the time of Paul's flight from Jerusalem. Within a year, Caligula had declared himself a god. As a part of this declaration, the emperor had ordered worship to be performed before his statues throughout the empire. As a consequence of this and therefore of major significance to the Sanhedrin, he had begun taking steps to have his statue placed in the Temple of Jerusalem.[1] The threat of this led the Jewish leaders to organize their opposition and this had taken all of the attention

---

[1]For understanding the full significance and impact of Caligula's acts for the Jewish leaders, see Cate, *A History of the New Testament and Its Times*, 225-26.

and energy of the Sanhedrin. They just did not have the time to devote to the problem presented by the followers of "the Way" at that time.

Furthermore, a rising tide of anti-Semitism throughout the empire had also called for the attention of the Jewish High Court in Jerusalem. The Jews themselves were becoming victims of persecution. Thus, their "problem" with the followers of Jesus had for a time simply faded into the background for the Jewish leaders.

The Church at Antioch

As a part of the ongoing spread of Christianity which we noted earlier, a congregation had been started in Antioch, capital of the Roman province of Syria. Up to this time, the new congregations that had been started by fleeing Christians had essentially been Jewish. At Antioch, however, the situation changed radically.

Some of the Jewish converts to Christianity in Antioch who were a part of the Diaspora began to witness to Gentiles, people who apparently had no prior connection with Judaism in any way. Being a part of the Diaspora meant that these Jewish Christians were very different from their companions who had come from Jerusalem and Judea, for they were quite familiar with Gentiles, having lived all of their lives in a Gentile world. As a consequence of those evangelistic efforts, converts were made from among the Gentiles of Antioch. When word of this development reached the leaders of the church at Jerusalem, they were greatly disturbed. Apparently wanting more information, they sent Barnabas to investigate, with the seeming intent that he report back to them on what was going on (Acts 11:20-22).

The choice of Barnabas may have been due to his background of being a part of the Diaspora himself, since he himself was from Cyprus (Acts 4:36). Furthermore, since he was a Levite, the disciples in Jerusalem would have been convinced that they could trust his Jewishness. Finally, being a Cypriot and of the Diaspora would have prepared him better to understand foreigners, or at least the people of the Diaspora.

However, when Barnabas arrived at Antioch and observed what was going on, although he rejoiced, he was also overwhelmed. Rather quickly he recognized that this new congregation needed help rather than investigation. It takes any investigator a great deal of courage as well as self-confidence to come to that kind of conclusion. In addition, he also realized that, in spite of his background, their ways of thinking and acting were just not natural to him. Barnabas immediately set his mind to the problem of finding someone who could handle the task better than he. Apparently the reputation of Paul's Tarsus-based ministry had reached Antioch, and so Barnabas set out to find this man who was already so effective at ministering to Gentiles, so that he might bring him to Antioch to assist in the ministry there (Acts 11:25-26). One of the marks of Barnabas's greatness was his willingness to find the best way to get a job done, even if it meant sharing leadership or even giving up personal authority.

We cannot be sure precisely when Barnabas brought Paul to Antioch. However, as we have seen, we do know that he and Paul were on a relief mission to Jerusalem when Herod died, and that Herod died in AD 44. Since we are told that Barnabas and Paul had ministered in Antioch "for a whole year" before the relief mission to Jerusalem (Acts 11:26-30), Paul must have arrived at Antioch at least as early as AD 43. Further, since any journey between Antioch and Tarsus, whether by land or sea, would have been difficult if not impossible during the winter, due to storms on the Mediterranean and deep snow in the mountain passes, Paul's arrival in Antioch most likely did not occur before March or April in AD 43. Admittedly, they could have arrived there in late AD 42, but this appears to be a bit too soon for other reasons, which we shall be forced to consider at a later time.

As we have also seen, Paul's ministry in Antioch was most likely not a new development in his life. Rather, it was apparently simply a geographic transfer of the activities he had already been carrying on in Syria and Cilicia from his home in Tarsus.

While Barnabas and Paul were in Antioch, the church there was warned or informed of a great famine in Jerusalem and Judea. Feeling compassion for the plight which this would obviously bring upon the community of Judean Christians, those in Antioch took up an offering to send to alleviate the suffering of the disciples in Jerusalem.

Such offerings and compassionate sharing appear frequently to have been characteristic of the churches that Paul started and where he ministered (Acts 11:27-30; 24:17; 1 Cor. 16:1-4; 2 Cor. 8:1–9:15; Rom. 15:25-28; Phil. 4:10, 14-18). It may have been characteristic of all the early Christian communities, but the only record we have of such compassionate concern comes from the Pauline churches.

In any case, this relief offering was carried to Jerusalem by Barnabas and Paul. The two emissaries seem to have arrived in Jerusalem just before Passover in AD 44 (Acts 12:3). About the time they arrived, a new persecution was directed toward the church by Herod Agrippa, who had James, the brother of John, and Simon Peter arrested. We do not know whether or not this renewed persecution was instigated by the Sanhedrin. At the very best, we can only hazard an educated guess. Perhaps it was taken on by Herod as just one more of the many attempts he made to win the favor of the Jewish leaders. In any case, Herod had James martyred soon after his arrest and imprisonment. In the meantime, Peter was held in prison until after Passover, with his execution being planned for the post-Passover period (Acts 12:1-4).

Luke gives no details relating to the events of the Jerusalem visit of Paul and Barnabas. The Jerusalem Christians were probably more concerned with the renewed assault by Herod than they were with the offering brought by the two companions. Furthermore, we must remember that this was Barnabas's first visit to Jerusalem since he had been sent to investigate what was happening with the church at Antioch and their ministry to the Gentiles. Apparently a report was neither given nor wanted. Perhaps this was due to the stress the church was enduring at the hands of Herod. They were simply more concerned with their own situation than they were with that of Barnabas and Paul. However, during their visit there, Herod died (Acts 12:20-23). For the Jerusalem church, the pressure of the moment was past.

Some time after that Passover, the two relief bearers left to return to Antioch, accompanied by Barnabas's nephew John Mark (Acts 12:25). (Note that, like Paul, John Mark also had a double name, one Jewish and one Roman.) Paul was never one to spend much time away from the mission activities he did so well. With nothing to do in Jerusalem and perhaps with the threat of renewed persecution eliminated for the moment, Paul, Barnabas, and now John Mark hurried back to the needs of the growing congregation of Antioch.

The Early Missionary Journey

Note that although they were eager to return to Antioch, Paul and Barnabas did not do so until "they had fulfilled their mission" (Acts 12:25). Luke's simple statement reveals a depth of commitment in Paul and Barnabas which all the rest of their lives exemplified. Furthermore, Paul demanded, or at least expected, no less a commitment from his companions in ministry. Total commitment to the service of Christ was for Paul the keystone of ministry. That was the kind of person Paul was and that was this kind of person he wanted around him and associated with him. Singleness of purpose was always, both before and after his conversion, one of the central features of Paul's character. So much so in fact, that he later wrote to his beloved friends at Philippi, "one thing I do, forgetting what lies behind and straining forward to what lies ahead, I press on toward the goal for the prize of the upward call of God in Christ Jesus" (Phil. 3:13-14). Urging the Philippians to this same commitment, he added, "Let those of us who are mature be thus minded" (Phil. 3:15).

Upon returning to Antioch, Paul and Barnabas once again joined the other leaders of that congregation in ministry. The names of those leaders reveal the extremely cosmopolitan nature of that congregation (Acts 13:1). "Simeon who was called Niger" was apparently a black man, as his nickname indicates. Although we do not know his homeland, it was apparently somewhere in Africa. Then there was "Lucius of Cyrene," a region on the Libyan coast of Africa which formed a Roman province with Crete. Lucius may either have been an African, a Roman, or of some other racial background of the Mediterranean world. Next came "Manaen a member of the court of Herod." Manaen is elsewhere identified as the half- or foster-brother of Herod.[2] What a man he must have been, coming to Christ from that background! And then the church of Antioch also had Barnabas and Paul as leaders. Both of them were a part of the Diaspora, Barnabas being from Cyprus and Paul being from Tarsus, and both were also intimately familiar with Judaism as it was practiced in Jerusalem.

As leaders of this growing Gentile church in Antioch, all of these men had already demonstrated their concern with the spread of the Gospel message. However, apparently during some special season of prayer, they and the church became convinced of two things. Their first conviction was that the Lord wished them to extend their efforts to a larger geographic area than just the region around Antioch. Their second conviction was that Barnabas and Paul were to be sent out as the initial agents of this mission (Acts 13:1-3). It is important to note that Luke always pointed out the part that the Holy Spirit played in the evangelism and mission enterprises of the church.

Following additional prayer and a service of commissioning by the church, Barnabas and Paul were sent away as the first "official" missionaries of the church. Insofar as Luke records, these were the first Christians to become involved in any church's *intentional* missionary enterprise. A major new dimension had been added to the activities, ministries, and mission of the church of Jesus Christ.

---

[2]See Archibald Thomas Robertson, *Word Pictures in the New Testament*, vol. 3, "The Acts of the Apostles" (Nashville: Broadman Press, 1930) 177.

When Barnabas and Paul set forth on what has come to be called "the first missionary journey of Paul," it does not really appear to have been a drastic change in ministry for either of them. Clearly, Barnabas had already been involved in the spread of the Gospel, the missionary enterprise of the church. Furthermore, if our reconstruction of Paul's so-called silent years is anywhere near correct, this was merely a new geographical direction for what Paul had already been doing in Antioch as well as earlier from his home in Tarsus. What was different was that this was an intentional act by a church, not merely a mission by an individual. For our purposes, it is still convenient to call this Paul's first missionary journey. However, I am convinced that such a title would have had little meaning for either Paul or Barnabas. It might be far more accurate and perhaps really more meaningful to call this "the church's first foreign mission."

Cyprus. When these two men set forth on their missionary enterprise, they took John Mark with them (Acts 13:5). The immediate destination of the missionary team was the relatively nearby island of Cyprus, Barnabas's homeland.[3] The first evidence of a missionary strategy on the part of Paul and Barnabas may be found here, for Luke records that they focused their ministry on the two major cities of Cyprus, Salamis and Paphos the capital.

Several other features which later show up as characteristic of Paul's missionary ministry show up in this first visit. The missionaries focused their attention upon major cities, the centers of population. Converts can only be made where people are. The missions in both of these cities were begun in the synagogues (Acts 13:4). When they faced opposition, they did not immediately flee from it, but confronted it directly.

In examining Paul and Barnabas's mission on Cyprus, we find at least three results that are significant for this study. First, we see that converts were made, including the proconsul Sergius Paulus himself (Acts 13:12). Paul almost always showed himself able to meet with and frequently to win

---

[3]For a more thorough understanding of the geographic and climatic influences upon the missionaries' travels, as well as for obtaining some knowledge of the archaeological evidence available from the places where they went, help can be found in Denis Baly, *The Geography of the Bible* (New York: Harper & Brothers, 1957); Cate, *A History of the New Testament and Its Times*; Bruce J. Malina, *The New Testament World*, 3rd ed. (Louisville: Westminster/John Knox Press, 2001); Herbert G. May, ed., *Oxford Bible Atlas*, 3rd ed. (New York: Oxford University Press, 1984); William M. Ramsay, *St. Paul the Traveler and the Roman Citizen*, 15th ed. (London: Hodder and Stoughton, 1926; repr.: Grand Rapids MI: Baker Book House, 1982); and Bo Reicke, *The New Testament Era: The World of the Bible from 500 B.C. to A.D. 100*, trans. David E. Green (Philadelphia: Fortress Press, 1968).

over people of power, distinction, and intelligence. Clearly, this does not mean that he was only concerned with such people. The overwhelming majority of his converts came from the ranks of ordinary people, or he would not have been able to establish the large number of congregations and churches that he left behind him.

The second significant result of the mission to Cyprus was quite personal for Paul. He started using his Gentile name, Paul, rather than his Jewish name, Saul. His later life shows that he never wished any of his own personal characteristics to hinder anyone from listening to and accepting his message. It is possible that he first made this transition to establish a common ground with the proconsul, Sergius Paulus himself, since they shared the same name. Paul was obviously willing to change whenever he could do so without compromise in order to share the good news of Jesus.

The third result of the Cypriot ministry was of perhaps the greatest ultimate significance, and this is that the missionary team apparently experienced a change of leadership. (This fact reflects most highly on the character of Barnabas, who was able to accept it with grace.) Up to the mission on Cyprus, the two missionaries are always referred to in Acts as "Barnabas and Saul" (Paul), with the name of Barnabas being given first as the apparent leader. The choice of Barnabas's homeland as the site of their first mission may also reflect his preeminence in both the planning and the mission itself. However, after the time they spent on Cyprus, we are told that "Paul and his company set sail from Paphos" (Acts 13:13). This phrasing leaves absolutely no doubt as to who was then in charge.

We have no way of knowing the chronology of the mission on Cyprus. Apparently Barnabas and Paul had returned to Antioch shortly after Passover, or even in mid- to late summer in AD 44. The question is whether or not they remained there for a brief or an extended period of time before beginning the missionary enterprise to Cyprus. If they remained in Antioch several months, they would most likely not have planned the voyage to Cyprus during the winter, for the storms in the northeastern Mediterranean during the winter made sea travel there most dangerous.[4] The two most likely times for their voyage to Cyprus would have thus been in the autumn

---

[4]The most thorough study ever done of sailing practices in the northeast Mediterranean during the first century AD is found in James Smith, *The Voyage and Shipwreck of St. Paul*, 4th ed. (London: Longmans, Brown, Green, Longmans, and Roberts, 1848). Although this is more than a century old, newer works either confirm the results of Smith's research or build upon it.

of AD 44 or in the early spring of AD 45, with the latter being the more probable given the time necessary to prepare for the journey.

For the same reason that their voyage to Cyprus is unlikely to have been in the winter, neither is it likely that Paul and Barnabas made the voyage northward from Cyprus to the mainland in the winter.

Luke compacts the mission on Cyprus into just nine verses in Acts. Further, in reading these, we get the impression that no great length of time was spent in either of the two cities upon which the missionaries concentrated their attention. Thus the mission to Cyprus could probably have been confined to three or four months, more or less. Therefore, if we date their arrival on Cyprus in early AD 45 we should probably date their voyage to the mainland in mid- to late summer of AD 45.

John Mark's Departure. Upon the arrival of the missionary team on the mainland in the region of Perga in Pamphylia, John Mark left Paul and Barnabas, returning to Jerusalem (Acts 13:13). We have no way of knowing the reason for Mark's departure, but Paul obviously considered it a desertion, a lack of (or change in) commitment on the part of the young man. To Paul, such was inexcusable, and this later served as the basis for a bitter disagreement between Paul and Barnabas (Acts 15:36-41).

Numerous conjectures as to the reasons for Mark's departure have been made, most of which malign Mark's character. In assessing these, we must not forget that the rift between Paul and Mark was later healed, for Paul wrote to Timothy near the end of his ministry, "Get Mark and bring him with you; for he is very useful in serving me" (2 Tim. 4:11).

Some suggest that Mark simply deserted the missionary team, finding the missionary task more difficult and their reception more hostile than he expected. Others suggest that he had simply become homesick for his family in Jerusalem. Yet others offer the opinion that the young man, being Barnabas's nephew, could not accept the fact that Barnabas had been superseded in the team's leadership by Paul. None of these suggestions appear to be likely, for very shortly Mark was ready to go with them again (Acts 15:37).

Further suggestions have been set forth that there was a personality conflict between Mark and Paul, or that the younger man became ill. Neither of these appears to be likely, for personalities don't change that radically and Mark and Paul were later able to work together in harmony. Furthermore, Paul himself experienced some kind of physical problem shortly thereafter and most likely would not have considered such a problem on Mark's part to have been an unforgivable desertion (Gal. 4:13-15).

One suggestion which is obvious enough to be recognized and yet has not been seriously set forth by scholars is that Paul and Mark began to disagree over their missionary strategy. Mark may have recognized that the congregations they were starting along the way needed something more left behind than simply the memories of the missionaries' words. Scholars generally agree that Mark's was the first of the four Gospels to be written. It is possible that it was at this time that Mark decided there ought to be something tangible, something setting forth their faith in writing, left behind for these new converts and their fledgling churches.[5] Paul disagreed, so the two separated, with Barnabas remaining with Paul. If this is the correct basis for Mark's departure, Paul later had to face the fact that he himself was wrong, for his new churches began to have problems precisely because they had nothing concrete, nothing written, to which they might turn for guidance when problems or difficulties arose. To compensate for that lack, Paul later was forced to write a number of letters for the purpose of aiding the congregations that he had started. Further, recognition of this error on Paul's part may explain why he later decided that Mark was "useful" to him.

However, the fact remains that, for whatever reason, Mark left Barnabas and Paul in Perga. Paul was disappointed, saddened, and angered by this "desertion," yet he and Barnabas kept on, committed to the task before them.

The Later Missionary Journey

Antioch of Pisidia. At this point, we are once again struck by the way the biblical narrative frequently makes events appear simple which, in actual fact, were quite difficult. After Mark's departure, Luke recorded that Paul and Barnabas "passed on from Perga and came to Antioch of Pisidia" (Acts 13:14). That journey was an unbelievably strenuous climb, ascending swiftly from sea level through rough and dangerous mountains to a height of about 3,600 feet. It led through the Taurus Mountains, a region subject to frequent flash floods. Further, it was a region generally inhabited by outlaws, bandits which even the Romans had not been able to eliminate.

---

[5]This idea was first suggested to me by Robert Overman, a dedicated Christian and a devoted student of the Bible in the First Baptist Church of Aiken, South Carolina. As the years have gone by, I have become more and more convinced that his idea is probably the right solution to our problem.

If our dating of Paul's arrival on the mainland at mid- to late summer of AD 45 is correct, his haste to get through these mountains would have been due to his desire to arrive at Pisidian Antioch before the normal early winter snows made the mountain regions impassable. The two missionaries would thus most likely have arrived at their goal of Pisidian Antioch by late autumn of AD 45. Ramsay's suggestion that Paul made this journey due to the fact that he had fallen victim to malaria and was seeking higher, dryer altitudes to recuperate hardly seems plausible.[6] No one suffering from severe malaria could possibly have undertaken such a difficult journey. More likely Antioch was chosen because it was a major city, a Roman colony, and situated upon the major east-west highway for travelers through the province of Galatia.

Upon his arrival in Antioch, Paul once again followed his two major missionary strategies. He went to a major city, apparently seeking through a mission there to influence the surrounding region. Further, he began his work there among the Jewish people, those who were already looking for the Messiah and who knew the working of God as revealed in the Hebrew Scriptures. On the first Sabbath following their arrival, he and Barnabas sought out the synagogue. As was customary in those times, visitors in the synagogue were invited to speak to the congregation.[7] Paul took that as an opportunity to share his message about Jesus.

Paul's Gospel message aroused no little stir among the Jews of the synagogue, so Paul and Barnabas were invited to return on the following Sabbath to share more of it (Acts 13:42-43). In the meantime, however, many of those who had heard Paul on that first occasion sought him out to learn more about those things of which he had spoken, not wishing to wait for the Sabbath. Apparently, they were so excited by his *kerygma* that they also went to their friends and neighbors, telling them about what they were hearing. When a great throng arrived at the synagogue on the following Sabbath, the local leaders were immediately filled with jealousy. This became the basis for conflict and opposition.

Finding rejection from the synagogue leaders, Paul turned to the Gentiles of the city. By them his message was welcomed and was spread

---

[6]Ramsay, *St. Paul the Traveler and the Roman Citizen*, 93.

[7]Rabbis were not found frequently in the regions remote from the environs of Jerusalem. Thus synagogue scripture study was generally the sharing of understandings and interpretations by the various men of the synagogue. Visitors offered an opportunity of ending the perhaps repetitive monotony of these services and also of hearing new ideas.

throughout the region. Apparently, the mission to Antioch was quite successful, so much so that the Jewish leaders conspired with "devout women of high standing" and the "leading men of the city" to organize a persecution of the two missionaries (Acts 13:50). This was neither the first nor the last time in history that agitators realized that the best way to get men to do something was to convince their wives first.

When that persecution arose, Paul and Barnabas were driven from Antioch. We are told that "they shook off the dust from their feet against them, and went to Iconium" (Acts 13:51). The Jews of that day had a custom, when they had traveled through Gentile territory or any religiously unclean region, of shaking off the very dust from their feet, lest they themselves be made unclean by its contamination. The sight of Paul and Barnabas doing this with the dust from the synagogue, as it were in reverse, would have been highly insulting to the Jewish leaders, for the missionaries would have been implying by their act that it was Jewish dust which was impure.

Iconium, Lystra, and Derbe. From Antioch, the missionaries journeyed next to Iconium, about ninety-six miles to the east of Antioch of Pisidia. This route required that they cross another major mountain range. Again, such a journey could not have been made during the season of the harsh winter snows. Although we have no way of knowing precisely how long Paul and Barnabas stayed in Antioch, they certainly could not (or would not) have left earlier than the spring of AD 46.

The reason for their selection of Iconium as the next place for their missionary efforts is unclear. Located a few miles off the major highway which ran from Antioch to Lystra, it was not nearly as accessible as either of those two cities. However, even though it was not on the major highway, Iconium was a trade center from which caravans moved eastward in several different directions. It may have been selected for this reason. As such, it would have furnished a natural starting point from which the Gospel could spread northeastward into the regions of Pontus and Cappadocia, being carried by the merchants to whom Paul and Barnabas preached.

Again, as was now Paul's well-established custom, the mission in Iconium was begun in the synagogue. This time, however, opposition arose more quickly. In spite of this, Paul and Barnabas remained there for a "long time," whatever that may mean. However, when the opposition became so strong that an attempt was made to abuse and/or lynch them (for this was what was intended by the stoning), they fled from Iconium to Lystra. This city was about twenty miles to the southwest and once again put them back on the main Roman highway.

Lystra was also a Roman colony and according to our records had few if any Jews there. With no synagogue in which to begin, Paul and Barnabas went directly to the Gentiles. This was their first opportunity insofar as we know for an "all-Gentile" mission.

According to Luke's records in Acts, Paul performed few miracles in his missionary journeys. However, he performed one at Lystra which backfired on him. The citizens there, seeing his healing of a cripple, assumed that he and Barnabas were gods come down to earth (Acts 14:8-22). Apparently the missionaries could not understand the people's local dialect and at first did not know what was happening as the crowds gathered quickly. However, when Paul finally became aware of the nature of the people's misunderstanding, things had gone so far that he was scarcely able to restrain the populace from offering sacrifices to the two missionaries.

Shortly after this, Jewish messengers arrived in Lystra and aroused the people to such animosity that they stoned Paul. This was clearly not a legal punishment but a simple case of crazed mob violence. Rather than blaming themselves for their misunderstanding of the identity of Paul and Barnabas, the people blamed Paul for misleading them. Such is the fickleness of popularity. In the stoning, Paul was knocked unconscious and was presumed to be dead (Acts 14:19). In these ancient cities, garbage was dragged outside of the city to be burned or fed to the scavengers. Thinking him to be dead, the people dragged Paul outside the city to get rid of his body. They were not even going to allow him the dignity of burial. Arriving as a missionary, welcomed as a god, he wound up being treated as garbage.

Fortunately, Paul was not dead. Upon regaining consciousness, he and Barnabas departed and went on to Derbe, a city about thirty miles further on to the southeast and on the same Roman highway. This journey was surely made slowly as a consequence of Paul's injuries. Less quickly than normal, they finally arrived at their destination. The beginning of the ministry in Derbe was again shaped by the absence of a Jewish synagogue. Thus Paul and Barnabas went immediately to the Gentiles. Apparently they were quite successful, making "many disciples" (Acts 14:21).

As before, in attempting to establish any sort of chronological framework for the mission in Iconium, Lystra, and Derbe, we are left wholly on our own, having only circumstantial evidence. For enough time to have passed for the ministries of Paul and Barnabas to have been successful and for the report of it to have spread so that opposition from other places pursued them must have taken most of the rest of AD 46. If we are correct in assuming that they remained in Derbe for the winter of AD 46/47, at least two things must have happened. First, regardless of whether our chronology is correct or not, they stayed in Derbe long enough for the Jewish opposition in other places to have died down. This may also probably have been due to the fact that they were now so far from any Jewish center. Further, with the winter over, they would once again have been able to travel through the mountain passes.

Thus, apparently in the spring of AD 47, Paul and Barnabas turned homeward, retracing their steps of the year before. On their way, they visited the churches they had established earlier, helping them to get better organized. We are told that in each place, "they . . . appointed elders" (Acts 14:23). The "elders" are most likely to be understood as having the same function as the elders of a synagogue, after which the early churches seem to have been patterned. These elders would have been administrative and spiritual leaders, old enough to be both wise and not easily swayed by fads.

The expression "appointed" comes from a Greek word meaning "to choose by a show of hands." Thus, while the missionaries led the churches to do their own appointing, they left the actual decisions to the churches, not taking that right upon themselves.

When they crossed back through the Taurus Mountains on their journey homeward, Paul and Barnabas stopped for a while in Perga of Pamphylia to preach the good news (Acts 14:25). They had apparently bypassed this city when they first arrived on the mainland, due to their apparent haste to get to Antioch before the winter weather set in. However, once again fearing the onset of the winter storms on the Mediterranean, they did not remain in Perga too long, soon going on down to the port city of Attalia. There they caught a ship bound for Antioch of Syria, finally arriving at their starting point in the autumn of AD 47. The entire mission seems to have taken about two-and-a-half years.

Given a joyous welcome by the church in Antioch, Paul and Barnabas reported on the success of their mission. The most striking feature of their report was that they had been establishing churches that were essentially Gentile. This news was received with joy by the church at Antioch. However, such news was not so joyous to others, especially to a group that had become active in Antioch. This group, centered in Jerusalem, believed no one could be a Christian who had not first become a Jew. They have come to be known as "Judaizers."

Paul and Barnabas remained "no little time with the disciples" at Antioch (Acts 14:28). During their absence from the church there, some of those Judaizers from Jerusalem who were disturbed over the spread of Christianity among the Gentiles, had come to that congregation with their proclamation that all Gentiles must first become Jews before they could become Christians. This meant essentially that all male Gentiles must be circumcised before they could become a Christian (Acts 15:1). (The rite of circumcision was the sign of the covenant by which males signified that they had become Jews.) These Judaizers were still in Antioch when Paul and Barnabas arrived.

It is possible that these Judaizers had arrived in Antioch shortly after the two missionaries returned. However, the idea that they had actually arrived earlier appears to be more likely. It is highly unlikely that these Judaizers would have made as much headway with their work if "the apostle to the Gentiles" had been present when they first arrived.

The controversy which arose between Paul and the Judaizers threatened to spilt the church. Not only that, it threatened to delegitimize the entire mission of Paul and Barnabas. Paul and Barnabas, as well as the entire church at Antioch realized that this was an issue that had to be settled and settled quickly. Once again Paul and Barnabas were selected as leaders, and a delegation was sent to Jerusalem for a conference upon the subject (Acts 15:2).

The Jerusalem Conference

The great conference at Jerusalem dealt with an issue that was at the very heart of the spread of the Gospel to the ends of the earth. It was one of the more pivotal points, if not the most pivotal point, in the early history of the church. Establishing both its relative and its exact date, if possible, is of prime importance.

I indicated earlier that it was most likely that this conference is to be identified with the second visit of which Paul wrote in Galatians:

> Then after fourteen years I went up again to Jerusalem with Barnabas, taking Titus along with me. . . . and I laid before them (but privately before those who were of repute) the Gospel which I preach among the Gentiles, lest somehow I should be running or had run in vain. (Gal. 2:1-2)

Although not specifically stated as such, the occasion to which Paul refers here appears to have been the same as the great conference described in

Acts 15. Paul was seeking reassurance that his mission was not based on false premises or assumptions.

From the standpoint of chronology, the problem at this point is that this visit was said to have been "after fourteen years." Paul had already written that he had gone to Jerusalem three years after his conversion (Gal. 1:18). As worded in the Greek, the fourteen years could be added on to the three years (and thus be in sequence) or could include the three years (and thus be in parallel), thus dating the visit fourteen years after his conversion.

Furthermore, as we have also noted, the three years could be two years and part of another or one year and parts of two others while the fourteen years could actually be thirteen years and part of another or twelve years and parts of two others. At the most, then, this visit could have been seventeen years after Paul's conversion. At the least, this visit could have been only slightly more than twelve years after that event. Considered from this perspective, the visit for the Jerusalem Council could have been as early as AD 46/47 or as late as AD 51. Various interpreters have placed it in most of the years between and including these dates.

For reasons that I shall point out in the following chapter, AD 51 is impossibly late, two or three years too late. I have chosen, as I indicated earlier, to assume that Paul's Galatian chronology is parallel, thus making the three years a part of the fourteen. If my reconstruction up to this point is anywhere near being correct, then this visit to Jerusalem would have been made in AD 48. This would have been fourteen years after his conversion, which fits with the Galatian reference. Further, it allows both the three and the fourteen to be interpreted in the same way. Since they are in the same basic citation, this is an absolute necessity.

The "three years" had to be interpreted as three full years in order to make any sense out of the reference to King Aretas of Damascus. It is inconceivable then that the "fourteen years" should not be interpreted in the same manner, making it fourteen full years. Further, this makes all of our calculations coincide with one another to this point. Thus we date the Jerusalem Conference in AD 48. Admittedly, I cannot *prove* that these assumptions are correct. But at least they work and this gives some assurance to their validity.

The issue before the Jerusalem conference was whether or not a Gentile had to become a Jew in order to become a Christian. To put it very bluntly, the ultimate issue was whether or not Christianity was ultimately only to be a sect of Judaism or whether it was to be freed from the constraints of Judaism to have its own independent existence.

From a faith standpoint it is easy to say that God would have seen that the two ultimately separated, regardless of what the Jerusalem conference decided. From a faith standpoint, I believe that to be true. However, from a historian's perspective, the question before the council was pivotal.

One of the noteworthy, though less important, features of this conference was that it was presided over by James, the brother of Jesus. He who had earlier been an unbeliever had now not only become a believer, he had risen to a position of leadership in the church of Jerusalem. When the council came into session, Peter, Paul, and Barnabas all made presentations. Although Luke did not specifically list any other presentations, we may be sure that spokesmen for the Judaizers also had their say. This was a matter of life and death to them also.

The final decision was set forth by James, declaring that they would not require Gentile converts to be circumcised. In other words, Gentiles did not have to become Jews to be Christians. However, the Gentile Christians were urged not to live in such a manner as to make their freedom offensive to their Jewish brothers (Acts 15:19-21). The point was that while Gentiles were free to become Christians without becoming Jews, *no Christian is ever free to trample upon or be offensive to the faith of other believers.*

Having made this monumental decision, the council immediately set out to inform the older Gentile churches (Acts 15:22-29). In listing those to be informed of this decision, no mention was made of the newer churches established by Paul and Barnabas on their missionary journey. Perhaps it was assumed that they were so far removed from Jerusalem that it was unnecessary, since they were already Christians and at the same time were probably not a real threat to the beliefs of the Judaizers. Further, James and the leaders in Jerusalem may have assumed that informing the home base of the Gentile expansion of their decision would take care of getting the word to their daughter churches. Be that as it may, the decision was received by the Christians of Antioch with great joy (Acts 15:30-31).

However, as is so often the case with decisions made by church councils, whether of major or minor importance, little was settled in actual practice. As we shall see in the following chapters, the Judaizers continued to be active, following Paul into his mission territories and creating problems for Gentile Christians wherever they went.

The Judaizers were simply not willing to accept the decision of the council. For them it was a matter of conscience. Viewed from our perspective, we know they were wrong, but they continued to press the matter for many years. As a consequence, their activities were a source of problems to Paul and many of the churches which he established throughout all the rest of his missionary ministry.

However, the issue was at least now officially settled. That being so, Paul, Barnabas, and the church at Antioch continued to proclaim their Gospel. After their return from Jerusalem, Paul, Barnabas, and the congregation of Antioch settled down to the task of ministering and witnessing to the people of Antioch (Acts 15:35). The year AD 48, which had begun with such controversy and trouble, passed away in peaceful evangelism and ministry.

Chapter 5

The Second Missionary Journey

Following the Jerusalem Council, Paul, Barnabas, and their companions returned to Antioch and settled down to a regular pattern of "teaching and preaching" (Acts 15:35). Once again we are made aware that neither Paul nor his friends saw themselves as missionaries only when they were on their specially designated missionary journeys. They obviously sought to share their faith continually, ministering whenever and wherever the occasion offered an opportunity, and often making opportunity when none presented itself.

Admittedly, the missionary journeys had to have been extremely strenuous physically, spiritually, and emotionally. But the Jerusalem Council and the journeys there and back were not without their stress either. Further, the ministry of the church at Antioch would have been stressful as well. The truth is that stress is always present in life and was certainly always present in Paul's life. In any case, while the return to Antioch was welcomed by Paul, the ministry following that return certainly gave him no time for rest or relaxation.

The Setting of Antioch

The city where Paul now ministered and which served as the base of his missionary endeavors deserves a brief consideration. A major north-south highway came through the Cilician Gates, the only pass of significance in the Taurus Mountains which blocked the way between Asia Minor and Syria. This highway led on to Antioch, from where it proceeded southward, leading on to Damascus and then proceeding southward into Palestine. At the point where this highway was crossed by the major east-west highway running from the port city of Seleucia to the Euphrates River and the great Mesopotamia Valley sat the city of Antioch in the province of Syria. Such a location made it one of the more important and cosmopolitan cities of the New Testament world.

Antioch of Syria was a city of great size, actually being made up of several smaller cities which had simply grown together. Only two or three other cities within the Roman empire were of comparable size and significance. Antioch certainly offered a large population to whom the Christians there could witness. Perhaps more importantly, it also offered an opportunity to share the Gospel with travelers, merchants, and soldiers who would carry it from there literally to the ends of the earth. Antioch was also the seat of the Roman government of the province of Syria, giving the

Christians there an opportunity of being far more influential than they could have been in many other cities.

Paul and Barnabas Disagree

In Antioch, therefore, Paul and Barnabas carried on their ministry of witnessing and preaching in the days following the Jerusalem Council. This for them was no time of rest and relaxation, but a period of continued ministry, even though the ministry there was clearly a change of pace. Paul, however, seems to have grown increasingly restless during this period. He had the world in his heart and apparently could never long remain in one place when he felt that the rest of the world so desperately needed to hear his message. These days in Antioch were apparently characterized for Paul by a growing impatience during the winter months when travel in that part of the world was difficult, if not impossible. However, as soon as the coming spring began to warm the earth, melt the snows, and still the Mediterranean storms, Paul truly began to feel the tug of the world leading him away from his immediate location.

Sadly, at this time a major dispute broke out between Paul and Barnabas, these two companions in mission. As they looked forward to and planned for new travels and new missions, Barnabas again wanted to take John Mark with them, giving him a second chance. Paul would have none of it. Knowing that Mark had deserted them once, Paul was convinced that they could not afford to risk another such failure from a member of their missionary team.

As is so often the case, a logical argument can be made for the position of both Paul and Barnabas. Barnabas was characteristically one who reached out in love to those who needed it. He had even done this for Paul when he had first arrived in Jerusalem following his conversion (Acts 9:27). On the other hand, Paul demanded of himself and other Christians a depth of commitment that allowed no room for wavering. Such a commitment, it could reasonably be argued, was absolutely necessary for anyone who would be a missionary.

As in most such arguments, there was really no right or wrong. What was really wrong was that as a result of this argument two old friends came to an angry parting of the ways. Barnabas took Mark and the two of them returned to the scene of their earlier mission on Cyprus. (Acts 15:39) So far as Luke was concerned, Barnabas and Mark not only sailed to Cyprus, they sailed out of the picture altogether. Neither one is mentioned again in Acts.

Paul, on the other hand, chose a new associate to be his companion, Silas or Silvanus and set out to return to the churches that he and Barnabas had started on the mainland in the northeastern part of the Mediterranean world (Acts 15:40-41). (Note that Silas is a nickname for or contraction of the name Silvanus.) In spite of the fact that it had come about due to a serious break in fellowship between the closest of friends instead of by a deliberate plan, the church at Antioch now had two missionary teams on the field.

Paul's choice of Silas as a new companion was probably influenced by several factors. First, Silas was a man in good standing with the Jerusalem church, having been selected as one of the emissaries to carry the decision of the great council back to Antioch and beyond (Acts 15:22). As a missionary, then, Silas would not be subject to the accusation of having the same bias toward the Gentiles that Paul had.

Second, Silas was a Roman citizen, as was Paul (Acts 16:37). This means that he would have been subject to the same legal protection as that to which Paul was entitled. Further, he could apparently write, an unusual skill in those times (1 Pet. 5:12). He, along with Timothy, later assisted Paul in writing the apostle's first letter to the church at Thessalonica (1 Thess. 1:1). He was obviously a skilled, mature Christian who was to become an excellent fellow laborer alongside Paul.

From Antioch to Philippi

Thus, most likely in the spring of AD 49 Paul and Silas set out from the church in Antioch to visit the churches that Paul and Barnabas had started on their first missionary journey. Two routes were open to them from Syrian Antioch to the cities of Derbe and Lystra. They could have traveled overland, following the north-south highway through the Cilician Gates, the major pass through the Taurus Mountains. Or they could have taken the shorter and quicker route, going by sea from Seleucia (Antioch's port city) to Tarsus, Paul's hometown. From there they would have traveled rapidly northward through those same Cilician Gates. Either way would have led them onto the plateau of southern Galatia through the pass in the Taurus Mountains.

The route they actually took to reach that point is relatively unimportant. However, the probability seems to fall on the side of the sea route as it would have been quicker and would also have allowed Paul to pass through Paul's home territory, a region which would have been quite familiar to him. Further, if, as we have suggested, Paul had started some churches in that region prior to his having been brought to Antioch, that route would have given him an opportunity to visit them as well as those he and Barnabas had started.

In either case, in the late spring or early summer of AD 49, as they stood upon the heights of the Taurus range, Paul and Silas would have at last gazed upon the regions where Paul had carried out most of his labors on that first missionary journey from Antioch. We can only imagine the eagerness with which Paul approached the sites of those former labors.

For Paul, the purposes of this return visit were both personal and official. First, he had to have been concerned with the welfare of those Christians and congregations he had left behind him there. He wished to know how they had prospered during his absence, or even if they still existed, having survived the hostility which the Jewish leaders had exhibited toward them. Second, he had probably been entrusted—or at least had been expected—by the Jerusalem Council to carry the decision of that council to these essentially Gentile churches. So he came joyfully to the scenes of his earlier labors with a message of freedom (Acts 16:4). It is possible that a letter from Jerusalem had already arrived with that message, but Paul would have felt a personal responsibility to share the decision with them himself.

Along the way, probably in the city of Lystra, Paul met a young convert whose reputation for faith and dedication had spread throughout the region. A relationship was begun between the great apostle and the young disciple which was to endure for the rest of their lives. The name of Timothy can hardly be mentioned without calling to mind the special relation he had with Paul, his friend and mentor. The apostle was so captivated by and attracted to the young man that Paul enlisted Timothy to accompany him and Silas on the remainder of their journey.

Before they moved on, however, Paul circumcised Timothy (Acts 16:3). This act on Paul's part is particularly striking, since just the year before he had fought so vehemently in Jerusalem to prevent such an act from being required of all Christian men. The historian must ask why Paul seems to have compromised his convictions at this point in his mission.

In seeking to understand Paul's act, we need to note that Timothy was more than merely a Gentile Christian. He had a Jewish mother and a Gentile father. Under the Jewish law at the time, such a child was illegitimate, and thus could not automatically be a part of the covenant community. On the other hand, being a half-Jew, Timothy's failure to be circumcised when he became an adult, his failure or refusal to intentionally become a convert to

Judaism as it were, might have been interpreted by some in the Jewish community as an outright rejection of their faith. Thus Paul performed the rite so that Timothy would not be a stumbling block to the very people with whom Paul always sought to begin his mission in each new community. Paul had refused to allow Titus to be circumcised since he was a Gentile. But Timothy's partial Jewishness was seen in a different light, and his lack of circumcision might have been an insult and thus become a stumbling block to other Jews.

We have no way of knowing how much time Paul and his companions spent in visiting Derbe, Lystra, Iconium, and Antioch of Pisidia. Clearly, they found the churches in those locations to be thriving. We know they remained among them for a while, ministering to them further and seeing continued growth in the numbers of converts throughout the region (Acts 16:5).

When they finished with that part of their mission, Paul was faced with the decision of where to go next, where next to share the Gospel. Apparently, he had planned on going to Ephesus, the capital of the province of Asia and one of the major cities of the Roman world. A mission to such a city would have fitted in ideally with his basic strategy of going to cities. However, in some way he became convinced that the Holy Spirit was not leading them to go in that direction, at least for the present (Acts 16:6). One major feature that must be noted about all of Paul's mission work was his sense that what he did or did not do was always guided by the hand of God's Holy Spirit.

Not knowing what to do after that rebuff, Paul and his party seemingly turned somewhat northward, intending to travel "through the region of Phrygia and Galatia" (Acts 16:6). Although Luke left us no record of what Paul and his companions did along the way, given Paul's passion for sharing the Gospel, he must certainly have preached as opportunities were provided as they went. However, we simply do not know whether or not he started any churches in that region. However, since Luke does not mention any, it is not likely that he did so.

Passing on up the eastern border of the Roman province of Asia, Paul, Silas, and Timothy finally came to the place where the province of Bithynia was situated to the north of them with Mysia being to their west. Paul regularly seems to have assumed that when you are traveling on mission, you keep going until you are forced to stop or change directions. He had therefore apparently assumed that since he could not go into Asia, he was to carry his mission northward into the Province of Bithynia. Once again, however, he became convinced that the Spirit of God had closed that door. Now what was he to do?

Rather than wringing his hands in dismay, Paul and his team stayed on the move, turning westward and traveling along the northern border of Asia and the southern border of Mysia. Although we are not told that Paul was refused permission by the Spirit to go into Mysia, the implication is clearly that this was so, for we are told that they passed by Mysia. Thus they finally arrived at Troas, located above the plains of Troy, a Roman colony on the border of the Aegean Sea. However, Troas possessed neither the size nor the economic and political significance of the any of the other places where Paul had started churches (Acts 16:8).

At Troas, Paul faced a major dilemma. He clearly believed that the Holy Spirit had not permitted him to carry his message of Jesus into the provinces to the north or south. Behind him, far to the east, lay regions which he had already visited. And at Troas, all that lay before him was the Aegean Sea. What was he to do? It seemed as if every door of ministry had been closed to him. The question of what he was to do and where he was to go seemed to be without any answer. During those long days and longer nights as he sought to understand God's purpose for him at that point in his life, he had a night vision, a dream, in which he saw "a man of Macedonia . . . standing beseeching him and saying, 'Come over to Macedonia and help us' " (Acts 16:9).

We must recognize that for Paul at Troas, the only way possibly open to him was the Aegean Sea with the province of Macedonia on the other side. Against that setting, four major suggestions have been made as to how his vision is to be understood. First, possibly going to sleep with the regions of Macedonia on his mind, Paul may in his dream simply have seen a typical Macedonian man, a representative from that area who was laying his people's needs before the apostle. Second, at this point in the narrative of Acts, a "we-section" begins which presupposes that Luke joined Paul and his team at that point (Acts 16:10). Luke was possibly from Macedonia and may have told Paul and his companions so much about his homeland that Paul dreamed about the physician and his stories.[1] Either of these suggestions are quite possible.

---

[1]Ramsay, *St. Paul the Traveler and the Roman Citizen*, 200ff., presents and defends this thesis.

However, the third and fourth suggestions appear to me to be more likely. In the Greek, the visionary figure of Paul's dream is described with the phrase, "a certain man of Macedonia," or "the man of Macedonia." Thus the expression seems to indicate that Paul saw a specific person from Macedonia who would have been well known by his companions. Luke would perhaps fit that criteria. But Paul was enough of a student and a historian to have known the history of the Roman province of Macedonia and its surrounding regions located across the Aegean Sea from where he lay.

Historically, Macedonia had been a region made up of numerous city-states until they were united by Philip of Macedon, the father of Alexander. It was Philip's dreams of greatness which were finally carried out by his son Alexander the Great. Even as Alexander had united the Mediterranean world in one empire, Paul may have envisioned Alexander calling him to come to his homeland and unite the world under one Gospel. Thus Alexander may have been the figure of Paul's vision.[2]

However, the most likely suggestion is that the subject of Paul's vision was Philip of Macedon himself. It was Philip's political vision that had united the city-states of Macedonia into a kingdom in the first place. And it was his goal that Alexander had carried out in the second place. Furthermore, Philip is referred to as "the man of Macedon" in contemporary literature. As Paul had been pondering over the regions beyond the sea from Troas, the only geographical region that appeared to be open to him, Paul the scholar would certainly have remembered and thought about the one who had united the cities there into the greatness that was Greece. During the night, Paul had dreamed of Philip, "the man of Macedon," who gave his life to unite his land. In that dream that great man had been pleading for Paul to bring to his land the message of life.

Paul wasted no time. Assuming that his dream had been the sign from God's Spirit for which he had been waiting, he and his companions set sail for Macedonia as soon as possible (Acts 16:11-12). This voyage of some 130 miles was apparently made in the wintertime, since the missionaries obviously took a coaster, a vessel which sailed among the many islands close to the coast, rather than taking the more direct route across the sea. Such a route was the only one possible in that season, for it was the only way affording any degree of protection from the winter storms. Merely making

[2]William Barclay persuasively presents this idea in *The Acts of the Apostles*, 2nd ed., Daily Study Bible (Philadelphia: Westminster Press, 1955) 131-32.

this journey in the winter shows the urgency with which Paul responded to his vision. If we are correct in our placing of this journey, then the voyage must be dated in the winter of AD 49/50. For the moment, we shall proceed on that assumption, which would mean that Paul and his companions probably arrived at the city of Philippi in early AD 50.

Philippi. Luke identified Philippi as the leading city of the district and a Roman colony (Acts 16:12). It had been named after Philip of Macedon, which may even further confirm the identity of the man in Paul's vision. He had gone to the one city of Macedonia which memorialized the one who had called to him for help.

When Paul arrived at Philippi, he discovered that the Jewish population of Philippi was not sufficiently large for them to have organized a synagogue. In such cities, the Jews who lived there frequently gathered at a riverside outside the city for their Sabbath worship. Thus Paul and his companions may have sought out such a place looking for just such a gathering. On the other hand, they may have asked about it in advance and known where they were going when they set out from the city itself.

Finding the gathering of Jewish worshippers for which they were searching, the missionaries shared their message about Jesus. The group they located seems to have primarily been made up of women (Acts 16:13). Among these was a woman named Lydia. She was a merchant and quite wealthy (Acts 16:14). In those days, it was most unusual for women to be merchants and was especially unusual for a Jewish woman to be such. Thus Lydia had to have been a person of great talent and drive to have made her way successfully in a man's world. Accepting Paul's Gospel, she opened her home to him and his team. Therefore they made it their base of operations for the rest of their stay in that city. It seemed that Paul and his companions were well situated for a long, peaceful, and successful ministry.

Appearances can be misleading, however, for trouble soon arose for Paul and Silas.[3] As the missionaries had gone about their mission in the

---

[3]Timothy is not mentioned either in the ministry at Philippi or in that which followed at Thessalonica (Acts 17:1-9). He next showed up as Paul departed from Beroea, leaving Silas and Timothy behind (Acts 17:14-15). We do not know if he was left behind in Troas, rejoining Paul later, or if he accompanied the team, simply missing the beating in Philippi and going unmentioned in Thessalonica. It seems more likely that, as he was new to the ministry, he may have been uninvolved in the episode with the slave girl in Philippi. At the very least, if he were with Paul and Silas in Philippi, he certainly was not viewed as a significant threat by Paul's enemies. Furthermore, given the nature of history writing in general and Luke's narrative in particular, he apparently went unmentioned in the

city, a slave girl with "a spirit of divination" began to cry out after them in mockery (Acts 16:16-17). The text literally says that she had "a spirit of Python." This would probably make her a servant of the Greek god, Pythian Apollo. His soothsayers were reputed to be ventriloquists and this slave girl may have been such. Her constant taunting led Paul to confront her as being demon possessed, and she was healed.

The healing of the young slave girl, however, created a problem for her owners, for she was no longer of value to them as a diviner and fortune-teller. They were enraged at losing the easy living derived from their exploitation of her condition, so these men had Paul and Silas charged before the magistrates of the city. Following a deliberate appeal to the prejudices of the magistrates by the accusers, Paul and Silas were beaten and imprisoned, even though the charges against them were quite false (Acts 16:18-24).

Confined in the inner prison, the missionaries were in too much agony from their beating to sleep, so they spent the night praying and singing. At this point an earthquake shook the prison, breaking off their shackles and shaking open the cell doors. When the earthquake awakened the jailer, he saw the devastation and was about to commit suicide, thinking that the prisoners under his charge had all escaped. Under Roman law, to have allowed prisoners under his care to escape was punishable by death. However, Paul intervened, assuring him that they were all there and using this as an occasion to share his message. As a consequence, the jailer and his household were won to this new faith, being baptized that very night.

On the following the morning, having decided that they had acted too hastily in their treatment of Paul and Silas, the magistrates sought to release them quietly. At this point, however, Paul informed them that he and Silas were both Roman citizens. This fact terrified the magistrates. Being a Roman colony meant that Philippi was entitled to a free self-government. At the same time, the rights of Roman citizens were protected throughout the empire, regardless. It was illegal anywhere in the empire to scourge or crucify a Roman citizen before he had been convicted of a crime.[4]

Realizing the real seriousness of what they had done the day before, the magistrates publicly apologized to the evangelists. However, the officials did ask them to leave the city, obviously wishing to be rid of them as soon as possible. Probably fearing another lynch-type scene, Paul and Silas

---

Thessalonian mission because he didn't fit into the main story.

[4]Robertson, *Word Pictures in the New Testament*, vol. 3, "Acts," 263-64.

visited the church they had started there briefly and then left Philippi (Acts 16:35-40).

Once again we are forced to make an educated guess as to how long Paul and Silas may have stayed in Philippi. Most likely it was about two or three months. It could not have been any less, for travel would not have been easy. This would place the end of the Philippian ministry in the early spring of AD 50. At the time when the spring weather made travel more practical, the Macedonian peninsula and its teeming cities opened up before them.

From Philippi to Athens

When Paul left Philippi for Thessalonica, he was surely at least accompanied by Silas, as the two of them were together when they later left Thessalonica together (Acts 17:10). Luke apparently remained behind, as the "we" material in Acts reverts back to a third-person narrative, a report of what "they" did (Acts 17:1). Timothy apparently also went with Paul and Silas, although he is not mentioned again in the Acts account until we are told that he and Silas were left behind in Beroea (Acts 17:14). At least if Timothy did not accompany Paul and Silas from Philippi, he had certainly rejoined them before they arrived in Beroea.

At this time a new missionary strategy of Paul's becomes apparent. From at least this time onward, Paul usually left a member of his team behind upon his departure from a church that he had started. This was clearly done when he was forced to leave sooner than he had planned. It was also apparently done to help the church get organized for ongoing ministry and proclamation.

Thessalonica. According to our chronological reconstruction, Paul most likely left Philippi and arrived in Thessalonica in the early spring, AD 50. He was apparently traveling on the major Roman highway that crossed the Macedonian Peninsula in an east-west direction called the Egnatian Way (*Via Egnatia*). On this journey he and his companions passed through both Amphipolis and Appolonia. These two cities divided the hundred-mile journey approximately into thirds. The missionaries apparently did not tarry to minister in either city, as their destination was the ancient city of Thessalonica.

Two facts suggest themselves as possible reasons for selecting Thessalonica as the next center for the efforts of the missionaries. First, a synagogue was located in Thessalonica. This kind of information would certainly have been shared with Paul by the Jews of Philippi. The missionaries were now far from the regions with which Paul would have been familiar from his home in Tarsus. Although he might possibly have learned the location of the major synagogues of the Diaspora from his rabbinic education in Jerusalem, it is far more likely that he was dependent upon learning these things from those with whom he was in touch along the way.

Second, even though Thessalonica was a free city within the Roman Empire with the power of self government, it did house the official residence of the governor of the Roman province of Macedonia. This would have made it a strategic location for Paul from which he could establish a mission to the surrounding region. Furthermore, we have already seen that Paul consistently seems to have welcomed opportunities of ministering where there was the potential opportunity of witnessing to governmental officials.

As usual, Paul began his ministry in Thessalonica in the synagogue. Once again, however, this resulted in some converts and a great deal of jealousy on the part of the synagogue leaders (Acts 17:2-7). Furthermore, as had almost become usual in such circumstances, a near riot seems to have occurred, although this time it outwardly had the appearance of being led by others than Jews, as the synagogue leaders employed some rabble-rousers to lead the attack against the missionaries (Acts 17:5).

Knowing that Paul had been staying in the home of a man named Jason in Thessalonica, the rioters went there looking for Paul and his companions, but failed to find them. In their frustration, they seized Jason and some of his companions, dragging them into the presence of the city rulers (politarchs), where they were charged with treason. While the rulers of the city were apparently not deceived by such charges, they were clearly disturbed at the breech of the peace by the attackers. If the charges of treason had been taken seriously by the city's rulers, the Christians would surely have been handed over to the Roman governor along with a recommendation for their execution, a sentence which, if acceded to, would probably have been carried out by crucifixion.

However the politarchs did make Jason and his companions post a bond (Acts 17:9). The terms of the bond are not given. At the very least, we may assume that they were prohibited from any act which might again contribute to such a breech of the peace. In other words, they were to cease and desist from any of their activities which "had turned the world upside down" (Acts 17:6). They may also have been told that they could no longer harbor Paul and his fellows, those outsiders who "had turned the world upside down." This latter suggestion appears to be the more likely, as the Christians of

Thessalonica immediately sent Paul and his fellow missionaries on their way (Acts 17:10).

A superficial reading of the Acts material seems to lead to the conclusion that the entire ministry in Thessalonica took only three weeks (Acts 17:2). However, a more thoughtful reading appears to indicate that, following the beginning of the rejection in the synagogue, the visitors carried their ministry to the Greeks (Gentiles), winning converts from among them. The "three weeks" apparently only applies to the length of their ministry in the synagogue. In either case, the opposition toward Paul, his companions, and his converts in the Thessalonian synagogue arose quite quickly.

Adding support to the idea that the ministry in Thessalonica was of some considerable duration is Paul's later message to the church at Philippi. In that letter Paul thanked them for their offerings that they had sent to him in Thessalonica on *two* different occasions (Phil. 4:16). For such to have occurred clearly requires a ministry considerably longer than three weeks. It is possible if Timothy had been left behind by Paul in Philippi that one of those offerings for Paul might have been delivered by Timothy as he rejoined the missionary team.

Beroea. Paul's ministry in Thessalonica must have lasted at least until summer, AD 50. Following that, he went to Beroea, a city located off the main highway, about fifty miles from Thessalonica and somewhat south of the Egnatian Way. If Timothy did not rejoin Paul at Thessalonica, he clearly did so here. More likely, however, he had come earlier. He would surely have known where Paul went following his departure from Philippi. Finding out where he had gone from Thessalonica would have presented significant difficulties. Given the size of Thessalonica, finding one of the few people there who would have known Paul's next destination would have been quite difficult, if not impossible.

The city of Beroea was relatively unimportant, having been called by Cicero an out-of-the-way town. Paul's mission in Beroea met with success both among the Jews and the Gentiles. Here he did not experience rejection from the rulers of the synagogue. To the contrary, he and his message that Jesus was the Christ received a thoughtful and willing acceptance.

However, word of the success of Paul's mission in Beroea eventually made its way back to the synagogue in Thessalonica. The jealousy of those leaders was once again aroused and they came to Beroea to once again stir up the crowds in opposition to Paul. This time the attack was apparently aimed only at Paul, so the Christians of Beroea helped him escape, leaving

Silas and Timothy behind (Acts 17:13-14). They escorted him to the coast to protect him from attack. There Paul and his protectors all got on a ship bound for Athens. The choice of escape by sea was apparently made due to their fear for his safety if he had traveled overland. The very fact that his escort from Beroea sailed with him indicates the seriousness with which they took their fear of an attack upon their new friend (Acts 17:15).

Apparently Paul and his escort had no idea of their ultimate destination when they left Beroea for its coastal harbor, some twenty-five miles away. Their intent apparently was merely to get on the first boat sailing for anywhere as a means of escape from his opponents in the region. Timothy and Silas remained behind to bring the mission work in Beroea to a close. However, since they had been left behind, they had to await word of where Paul was before they could leave to rejoin him. Thus they had to await the return of Paul's escort.

The ministry in Beroea was clearly of an extended duration. Most likely Paul's forced departure would have been in the early autumn, AD 50. It could possibly have been a bit later. The fact that they took a ship to Athens may mean everything or nothing. If it were time for the onset of the winter storms, Paul was far too experienced a traveler to have set forth on a voyage into the deep sea. However, a coastal vessel, staying within the shelter of the countless islands along the coast of Macedonia would have offered relative security. In addition, Paul may simply have been desiring to proceed further in the same general southerly direction in which he had already been traveling.

In any case, it appears that Paul had not originally intended to carry his mission into the province of Achaia, where Athens was located. He seems at first merely to have intended to wait there for his companions to rejoin him before he decided what to do or where to go next. However, for a person with Paul's sense of missionary commitment, that was not to be.

Athens. At that time, Athens was the intellectual center of the world. It was the place where young men who wished to be numbered among the Roman world's intellectual elite went to study. While neither the national nor the provincial capital, Athens probably possessed the greatest influence of any city at that time over the thoughts of the entire Roman empire. Further, most of the ancient world's religions could be found in Athens. It was this latter situation which finally seems to have provoked Paul to preach his Gospel (Acts 17:16).

In Athens, Paul preached both in the synagogue and in the marketplace (the *agora*). In the agora Paul attracted the attention of some of the

Athenian philosophers who wanted to hear more of what he might have to say, although their desire apparently did not arise out of a sincere interest. Rather they seem to have merely been seeking for intellectual stimulation, as it were, playing rhetorical and philosophical games rather than engaging in a genuine quest for knowledge.

Apparently being a student of philosophy from his Tarsus background, Paul approached his audience at Athens using their own methods, appealing to their intellect. However, when he first spoke to them of the "resurrection," the Athenians thought he was speaking of a female goddess who was the consort of a god named Jesus. However, when his audience finally realized that he was speaking of Jesus being raised from the dead, many of them began to mock him for such a foolish idea (Acts 17:18, 32). The Athenian philosophers were quite aware that people simply do not rise from the dead.

In addressing the philosophers of Athens, Paul demonstrated another part of his missionary strategy. Seeing an altar on Mars Hill dedicated "To an unknown god," he set out to explain who this God was. His obvious strategy was to begin his proclamation in a manner and with a subject with which his audience could identify (Acts 17:23). This missionary strategy has been adopted by most major Christian missionary organizations during the second half of the twentieth century.

Some interpreters describe Paul's mission in Athens as if it were wholly unsuccessful. That is simply not so, at least insofar as Luke reports it. While he may not have enjoyed the same success there as he had experienced in Beroea and other places, he did see a number of converts result from his Athenian ministry (Acts 17:34). Furthermore, although he did not leave behind him large numbers of converts, Paul's Athenian ministry can no more be called ineffective than that in several other places which he had visited earlier.

Paul's detractors have pointed to his words later written to Corinth as bearing testimony to the fact that a carefully reasoned, philosophical sermon was not an effective way of presenting the Gospel. Such interpreters claim that Paul had learned through a bitter experience at Athens the vital lesson that he should never try merely to reason people into the kingdom of God. They believe that his words to the Corinthian congregation set forth in no unmistakable terms this lesson which he had learned in Athens.

> When I came to you brethren, I did not come proclaiming to you the testimony of God in lofty words of wisdom. For I decided to know nothing among you except Jesus Christ and him crucified. And . . . my speech and my message

were not in plausible words of wisdom, but in demonstration of the Spirit and of power, that your faith might not rest in the wisdom of men but in the power of God. (1 Cor. 2:1-5)

Such an interpretation might possibly be correct. But it is not necessarily so and most likely is wrong. First of all, given the sinful, false sophistication of the people of Corinth, Paul may have simply decided upon his arrival that his proclamation in that location had to be simple and straightforward. In Corinth, as in other places, he was simply adopting a purposeful presentation designed and intended to be the most effective one possible in that location. These words would then have been simply a specific application of his basic affirmation to those same Corinthians that "I have become all things to all men, that I might by all means save some" (1 Cor. 9:22).

Second, to believe that the man who later penned some or all of Romans, Colossians, and Ephesians would be claiming that a carefully reasoned, philosophical approach to the Gospel was inappropriate requires more imagination than I can achieve. To the contrary, all of Paul's epistles, and especially those of his more mature ministry reveal the very opposite approach. True, he kept his focus upon the crucified Christ. But he always presented the implications and ramifications of that event in carefully reasoned, thoroughly philosophical terms. Further, on at least five different occasions he set forth his premise that there was no place for and no excuse for ignorance among believers (Rom. 11:25; 1 Cor. 10:1; 12:1; 15:34; 1 Thess. 4:13). A man who made such emphases surely did not turn his back upon carefully reasoned sermons which addressed audiences in their own vocabulary and thought patterns.

Thus I conclude that Paul's words to the Corinthians were not a denial of the validity of the approach he had used in Athens. To the contrary, they were an affirmation of his basic strategy that the approach to each audience had to be designed and tailored for that audience alone.

One of Paul's converts in Athens was "Dionysius the Areopagite" (Acts 17:34). Dionysius was a member of the Areopagus, the high court of Athens, and according to an early church historian named Eusebius, Dionysius later became the first bishop of Athens, ultimately dying as a martyr for his faith.[5] The church of which Dionysius was bishop and the man who became its bishop both stand as living monuments to the vital success of Paul's Athenian mission.

---

[5]Robertson, *Word Pictures in the New Testament*, vol. 3, "Acts," 293.

Timothy and Silas obviously rejoined Paul shortly after he himself had arrived in Athens. After the protective escort from Beroea had gotten him to Athens, they had returned home, at which time they obviously had informed Paul's two companions where they might locate their friend and mentor. As soon as Timothy and Silas joined him, however, wanting news from the congregations he had been forced to abandon so hastily in Macedonia, Paul sent Timothy to Thessalonica and apparently sent Silas to Philippi (1 Thess. 3:1-2). Paul himself soon left Athens, going on to Corinth where both of his companions later rejoined him (Acts 18:5).

In trying once again to establish a chronology for Paul's mission, we are forced to make an educated guess when we seek to determine how long Paul may have stayed in Athens. The ministry there was peaceful, but does not appear to have been of an extended duration. Perhaps the best estimate is that Paul left Athens and arrived in Corinth in the latter days of AD 50.

From Corinth Back to Antioch

Corinth. In Corinth, Paul began a ministry in what was reputed to be the most wicked city of the New Testament world.[6] Corinth's reputation for evil was known throughout the Mediterranean environment. To call someone a "Corinthian" in the Roman world was the height of insult. All this would certainly have been known to a thoughtful, informed youth growing up in the Roman city of Tarsus. It would just as surely have been known to any rabbinic student in Jerusalem who was part of and concerned with the Diaspora.

Corinth was a Roman colony, situated on a narrow isthmus in the province of Achaia. That strategic location determined both its economic importance and its cosmopolitan nature. In order to avoid the dangerous storms at the tip of the Macedonian peninsula, many ships were unloaded on one side of the Corinthian isthmus, their cargo carried across to the other side where it was reloaded on other ships whose cargo had been carried in the opposite direction. Small ships were actually hauled out of the water, placed on logs as rollers, and pulled across the isthmus. This in itself required large numbers of people to serve as laborers and overseers. Obviously such operations required a fairly major city and business center to feed, house, and clothe all those involved in such enterprises. In addition, the sailors who had to wait while such labors were carried out also searched

---

[6]Joseph A. Callaway, "Corinth," *Review and Expositor* 57/4 (October 1960): 381-88.

for the kinds of things sailors frequently search for when they come to land after having been at sea for an extended period. This in turn required additional housing and businesses. To meet these needs the city of Corinth had been founded. In meeting these needs, it had prospered.

In Paul's day, the city of Corinth was the Roman capital of the province and therefore housed the governor. Because of the many merchants and seafaring people from all over the world who had become connected with the city, a large variety of religions flourished there, numerous shrines dotted the city, and multiple gods and goddesses were worshipped there. The chief goddess of Corinth, however, was Aphrodite. The priestesses in her temple were little more than sacred prostitutes and the worship involved the worshippers having sexual intercourse with those priestesses in the temple. Such an evil and immoral city offered a prime target for Paul's message of Jesus. Perhaps because of this need and opportunity, he stayed there longer than any other city he had visited to that point in his missionary activities.

When Paul had first arrived in Corinth, he met two people who were to become both his close friends and his associates in ministry: Priscilla (sometimes called by the diminutive nickname Prisca) and Aquila. Several things about them are significant. First, they are described as Jews who had been driven out of Rome by Claudius (Acts 18:2). An external validation of this reported expulsion is given by the Roman historian Seutonius, who reported that riots had broken out among the Jews in Rome instigated by one "Chrestus."[7] This is apparently a Latinization of the Greek word *Christos*, which means Christ. Some Christians apparently had come to the synagogue in Rome, witnessed, won converts, and then been faced with the same kind of opposition and disturbance that Paul had faced in other synagogues in other cities.

In fact, Claudius did not order the Jews to leave Rome. He only forbade their meeting together. However, for the Jews, such an edict would have forced all those committed to the worship of God to leave the imperial city. Among those who did so were Priscilla and Aquila. Since they were in Corinth when Paul arrived, they must have left Rome at least as early as the autumn of AD 50. They could obviously have departed earlier. This would

---

[7]Robertson, *Word Pictures in the New Testament*, vol. 3, "Acts," 295.

fit well, for Roman historians date the edict of Claudius as having been issued about AD 49.[8]

These two new friends of Paul were apparently already Christians, as no mention is made of their conversion. Further, they were tentmakers, the same trade as that of Paul (Acts 18:3). This, coupled with their common faith, led them to welcome Paul into their home. The fact that they had a home large enough to do this suggests they were people of some means. They also would have had a steady income from such a business, for a constant need existed in Corinth for tentmakers or sailmakers to furnish the necessary sails for all the vessels which traded there.

As usual, Paul once again began his ministry in Corinth at the synagogue. However, when the Jews rejected him and his message, again as usual, he turned his mission to the Gentiles. This time he moved his worship services from the synagogue into a house just next door, the home of a man named Titius Justus (Acts 18:5-11). Such a location would have been a tremendous insult to the Jews in the synagogue. By being located adjacent to their place of gathering and worship, they were forced to see the Jewish converts, the Gentile converts, the other Christians located there like Priscilla and Aquila, and those merely seeking to hear Paul's message, coming and going regularly. To add injury to insult, during this time the president of the synagogue himself, Crispus, accepted Paul's Gospel and became a Christian. Thus seeds were being sown for a harvest of bitter discord between the two groups. The Jewish leaders of Corinth, however, exercised more patience than their fellows had done elsewhere, biding their time for an appropriate opportunity in which to act. While this situation dragged on, Paul continued to minister there for a period of eighteen months, essentially being left alone by his enemies (Acts 18:11). If our chronological reconstruction so far is correct, this brings us to mid-summer, AD 52.

At this point we discover that, just as we had suspected, the Jewish leaders of Corinth had not been acquiescent in the face of Paul's successes but had merely been waiting for the right opportunity to act. When Gallio was named proconsul of Achaia, that time came and they lashed out at Paul with a vengeance (Acts 18:12-17).

Our chronological reconstruction suggests that Paul was brought before Gallio in mid-summer, AD 52, which obviously fits with what we know about Gallio's reign from AD mid-51 to AD mid-52 (or from AD mid-52 to

---

[8]Robertson, *Word Pictures in the New Testament*, vol. 3, "Acts," 295.

AD mid-53). Admittedly, as we have sought to establish dates for this part of Paul's ministry, we have made numerous assumptions as to lengths of ministries and times of travel. However, the fact that our assumptions have suggested a date for Paul's appearance before Gallio at a time which fits in with the known chronology of Gallio at least gives some affirmation as to the validity of some if not all of the assumptions we have made.

Gallio was well aware of the recent troubles with the Jews with which the Emperor Claudius had been forced to deal. At that time, official Rome perceived Jewish leaders as troublemakers. Thus Gallio simply dismissed their case against Paul, refusing to deal with it in any manner.

Shortly after Paul's case was so abruptly dismissed by Gallio, some group in the city seized Sosthenes, the new ruler of the synagogue, and beat him (Acts 18:17). Whatever group this was, they had apparently interpreted Gallio's decision as giving them freedom to express their anti-Semitism with openness and violence. The very fact that the new governor seems to have ignored this breach of the peace shows that they were correct in their judgment. Paul later associated himself with a man named Sosthenes in a letter to the Corinthian church (1 Cor 1:1). If this is the same man, apparently he had later become a Christian.

During Paul's long stay in Corinth, he added a new dimension to his missionary ministry. Apparently for the first time he began to write letters to the churches he had established. Although travel was not easy in the ancient world, letters and information moved between various parts of the Roman Empire with a great deal more speed and ease than we might ever have imagined. Thus Paul heard from his scattered congregations and was able to communicate with them with relative ease.

During Paul's stay in Corinth, he appears to have written Galatians and 1 and 2 Thessalonians. (He may also have written other letters that have not been preserved.) Galatians was written because he had received word that some among the congregations of Galatia had been led astray by Judaizers. Paul was incensed at this, for this issue had supposedly been settled at the Jerusalem Conference. Writing to the Galatians in no uncertain terms, he asserted,

> I am astonished that you are so quickly deserting him who called you in the grace of Christ and turning to a different gospel — not that there is another gospel, but there are some who trouble you and want to pervert the gospel of Christ. (Gal. 1:6-7)

Following his denunciation of what they had done, Paul placed a major emphasis on the unmerited grace of God and the freedom which being a Christian brings to every believer.

Furthermore, remembering the haste with which Paul had left Thessalonica, fleeing from persecution, it is obvious that he had not had any opportunity to bring his mission there to a close, helping the congregation get organized to minister. Timothy had been sent back to find out how they were getting along and had now rejoined Paul in Corinth, bringing good news about the conditions of the church in that city. The congregation there was apparently now enjoying peace. Upon receiving that news, Paul wrote to the church expressing his gratitude and clarifying a matter or two about which they appear to have been uncertain.

However, sometime thereafter Paul received additional news from Thessalonica which he found less encouraging. Apparently his sermons along with some of his words in the first letter about the nearness of the time of the return of the Lord Jesus had been misunderstood. Some among the congregation had been so convinced that Jesus was about to return to earth that they were merely gathering together in worship as they waited for the great event. Although Paul reaffirmed his belief that Christians should expect the return of Jesus at any time, he also asserted bluntly that Christians must go on with life while they wait, writing quite forthrightly to them, saying, "If anyone will not work, let him not eat" (2 Thess. 3:10).

As we read these letters, we find no indication that Paul had any idea that he was writing what was later to become sacred Scripture. He was simply expressing pastoral concern for the people in his churches.

It is noteworthy that Paul associated Silas and Timothy with him when he wrote to the church in Thessalonica. They were not so associated in his letter to the Galatians. This leads me to conclude that Galatians was probably written first before the two companions had joined Paul in Corinth. The Thessalonian letters would then have been written after the team was reunited.

Back to Antioch. Following his judicial hearing before Gallio, Paul remained in Corinth "many days longer" (Acts 18:18). This would probably bring us to the late summer or early fall of AD 52. Then he and his companions set sail from Cenchrea, the port of Corinth, journeying directly across the Aegean to Ephesus. Choosing this route was most likely due to the fact that he could not get a ship going directly to Caesarea, the port of his ultimate destination. However, this choice may have been due to the fact that he still wanted to carry out a ministry in Ephesus. In any case when they stopped, he briefly visited with the synagogue in Ephesus. Although asked to remain longer by the Ephesian elders, he declined. However, when he departed he did leave Priscilla and Aquila behind.

Paul's haste to depart from Ephesus probably meant that they were near the end of the sailing season of AD 52. Postponing his journey to Caesarea would have meant that he would have had to spend all winter in Ephesus. He and his companions quickly took another ship, sailing onward to Caesarea. From there they hurriedly traveled to Jerusalem. His visit to that city and the church there indicates that Paul continued to be both a good Jew and to acknowledge the significance and prominence of the Jerusalem congregation. Fulfilling his obligations there, Paul finally turned northward, apparently arriving at Antioch in late AD 52. We may assume that he was welcomed with joy by a congregation eager to hear of his new accomplishments for the Lord.

This homecoming brought Paul's second missionary journey to an end. He had originally started out to revisit the congregations of Galatia with the apparent intent of going on to Ephesus for a major ministry. Instead, he had gone in a different direction, starting churches in Macedonia and Achaia. The significance of this was that Paul had moved his mission from the continent of Asia to that of Europe. It is ridiculous to suggest, as some have done, that if Paul had not gone in this new direction that Christianity would have remained an Asian religion. We have seen that Christianity had already spread to Rome itself long before Paul ever got there. The Gospel was already in Europe before Paul went to Philippi. At the same time, however, with Paul's crossing of the Aegean Sea he had added a European dimension to his personal mission. We dare not minimize that change for him.

In a very real sense, as long as Paul was preaching in Asia, he was a *home* missionary. That was his own territory and he was among people with whose culture he was personally familiar. When he crossed to Macedonia, however, he truly became a *foreign* missionary. In addition, whether or not John Mark had thought of it first, during this journey Paul had realized the necessity for committing important things to writing for his churches. What we have come to know as the New Testament had its beginnings during this trip.

Chapter 6

The Third Missionary Journey

Few people have been privileged to accomplish as much as Paul did in his missionary activities over the time span of approximately eight-and-a-half years which covered his first two missionary journeys. Setting sail with Barnabas in the spring of AD 43, Paul had embarked upon a mission that resulted in churches being planted throughout the northeastern Mediterranean world, in five Roman provinces—Galatia, Cilicia, Asia, Macedonia, and Achaia—and on two continents—Asia and Europe. When he returned to Antioch in the fall of AD 52, he had every reason to be both pleased and exhausted. He should have been pleased with what he had accomplished and exhausted because of the labors and hardships he had endured. He had left churches behind him everywhere he had gone. At the same time, in doing this, he been imprisoned, persecuted, and forced to flee the scene of his ministry on numerous occasions.

In a day when most people seldom traveled more than a few miles from home, Paul had covered several thousand miles on foot. He had also covered an additional several thousand miles in several sea voyages, not the safest means of transportation as is attested by the remains of the hundreds of wrecks from that era that have been discovered scattered over the bottom of that region of the Mediterranean by undersea archaeologists.

If ever a man deserved an extended period of rest, it was Paul at the end of that second missionary journey. This, however, was not to be. As noted in the preceding chapter, Paul had discovered that some of the churches he had started in Galatia were having difficulties with people who were perverting the Gospel. Although Paul had already written to these churches, he wanted to visit them personally in order to see how they were getting along.

Moreover, Paul still had two great longings in his life. Never one to rest on the accomplishments of the past, he was always pressing on to new opportunities and challenges. He urgently wanted to minister in the cities of Ephesus and Rome. On his journey homeward from Corinth at the end of his second missionary journey, he had promised the elders from the synagogue at Ephesus that he would return to them if God willed (Acts 18:20-21). He also later wrote to the church in Rome expressing his eagerness to minister there (Rom. 1:9-15). These two great cities of the empire had taken root in his heart as the next focal points of his ongoing mission. New challenges awaited. New opportunities beckoned.

The Mission in Ephesus

Probable Chronology. And so, sometime after this homecoming to Antioch of Syria, and after spending only a brief time there, Paul once again set out on a new missionary enterprise. For the same reasons we have noted before, reasons centered on the difficulties of travel on both land and sea in the northeastern Mediterranean region during the winter months, it is most likely that Paul began this new expedition in the spring of AD 53 following his return home in the fall of AD 52. This would most likely have been as early as Paul would have deemed it safely possible. This third missionary journey began with the purpose of initially visiting the churches that he had founded in Galatia.

We do not know whom Paul took with him as missionary companions when he left Antioch. When he visited Ephesus the preceding fall and left Priscilla and Aquila there, he had most likely sent Timothy on to visit the Galatian churches at that time. This becomes even more likely when we remember that Timothy's home was in the Galatian region. Thus that mission would have been as much a homecoming for Timothy as going to Antioch was for Paul. Furthermore, Paul was more and more using emissaries to go to places when and where he could not go himself. This, too, would give a basis for sending Timothy to Galatia. So it was that he and Timothy were probably reunited in the Galatian region in the early days of this third mission trip. However, Paul seems never to have set out alone from anywhere unless persecution forced him to do so, thus he had also probably taken some companion or companions in ministry along with him from Antioch as he began this journey. Their identity remains obscured by the mists of time.

Paul was seeking to do at least two things on this third visit to the Galatian churches in the spring of AD 53. First, he was seeking to strengthen them in the faith. Their beliefs had apparently been wavering in the face of the pressures of the Judaizers. If possible, Paul wanted that issue settled once and for all. In addition, Paul may also have been seeking a direct confrontation with those whom he, as well as the church in Jerusalem, had concluded to be grossly wrong in their understanding of the Gospel. To achieve these two goals would surely have taken more time than he had spent in that region on his second visit to those churches in AD 49.

Furthermore, apparently during Paul's brief visit to Jerusalem at the end of his second mission trip in AD 52, he had become aware of the financial need in the Jerusalem church. During the winter and the early spring, he had apparently decided that one of the better ways to solidify the larger Christian community as well as to demonstrate its interrelatedness was to lead the new churches to send an offering to relieve the plight of the people in the church of Jerusalem. Paul obviously spent some time during this third visit to Galatia getting things organized for the receipt and disbursement of this offering (1 Cor. 16:1-2).

By the time he finally completed his mission among the Galatian churches, Paul seems to have added Timothy to his party. Then he and his team headed for Ephesus (Acts 19:1). At long last he was going to be able to minister in that strategic city. Ephesus was one of the more important centers of commerce in the Roman Empire. In addition, it was renowned for its temple dedicated to the worship of the goddess Artemis. This temple was reputed to be one of the seven wonders of the world.

The date of Paul's arrival in Ephesus is uncertain, being dependent upon the length of his visit in Galatia and the time spent in journeying onward from there. The need in Galatia was great, and the apostle could have stayed through the entire summer and well into the fall. However, unless he also spent the winter there, he would certainly have planned on getting through the mountain passes separating him from the province of Asia before the winter snows set in. Furthermore, his major goal on this trip from the outset seems to have been Ephesus, so he would certainly have been in a hurry to get there as soon as was reasonably possible. Most likely therefore Paul would have tried to arrive in the great city of Ephesus in the late fall or early winter of AD 53.

Between the time Paul had left Priscilla and Aquila in Ephesus and the time that he actually arrived back there, that city had been visited by a preacher named Apollos, an Alexandrian Jew who was also a Christian (Acts 18:24-28). Apollos was a man of great learning and eloquence, and was a thorough student of the Jewish Scriptures (the Old Testament). Being an educated Jew from Alexandria, he was probably a disciple or follower of Philo, the great Jewish philosopher of that city. That means that he would most likely have been immersed in that man's allegorical approach to the interpretation of the Scriptures.

While oratorically quite effective in proclaiming the Gospel, Apollos was lacking in some areas of his faith. First, he had only experienced the baptism of John, not Christian baptism. We are left uncertain about what else he lacked, except that we are told that Priscilla and Aquila helped to correct him (Acts 18:25-26). If, as we have suggested, Apollos was an allegorist, perhaps they showed him a better way of understanding and interpreting the Scriptures. Luke has left us no record that Priscilla and Aquila suggested that the faith of Apollos was inadequate enough that he needed to be baptized again, as some have suggested.[1]

When Apollos finished his mission in Ephesus, he had decided to cross over to Achaia, perhaps with the intent of bringing his Alexandrian Jewish philosophy into confrontation with the Greek philosophy of Athens. At that point, however, Priscilla and Aquila gave him letters of introduction to believers whom they had known in Corinth and sent him on his way. Upon his arrival in Corinth, the former home of Priscilla and Aquila, Apollos again began to proclaim his message. His eloquence and effectiveness led some of the Corinthian Christians to compare him with Paul while others compared him with Simon Peter. This comparison unfortunately led to the growth of factions within the church there (1 Cor. 1:12).

In the meantime, Paul at last arrived in Ephesus. Reconstructing Paul's mission in Ephesus requires a great deal of biblical detective work, drawing inferences both from Luke's narrative in Acts and from Paul's own epistles. Further complicating this effort to unravel the details of Paul's Ephesian ministry is the fact that he was also involved during at least part of this time in a long-distance ministry with some of his other churches, particularly the one in Corinth.

The basic format of Paul's ministry at Ephesus followed that of his other missions, beginning with his usual approach to the Jewish synagogue. This part of his Ephesian mission continued for about three months, a bit longer than usual, before trouble broke out (Acts 19:8-9). As a specific missionary strategy, the synagogue ministry at Ephesus was probably unnecessary, for Priscilla and Aquila and probably others had already established a Christian congregation there. However, Paul had earlier promised the synagogue leaders that he would return to share his message with them, and he did so (Acts 18:19-21). We can safely assume that Paul also worked with the Christian congregation during this initial period of his ministry in that city. It is inconceivable that he would have ignored them during this time. These initial days of Paul's ministry in Ephesus probably extended into the early months of AD 54.

---

[1]Paul's later experience of rebaptizing some Ephesian disciples since they had only received John's baptism has been used by some as a basis for suggesting the same for Apollos. There is no reason either suggested or implied in the New Testament for leading us to draw that conclusion.

However, Paul's preaching to the Jews in Ephesus ultimately had the same result that similar efforts had produced elsewhere. Opposition arose and eventually he became unwelcome in their synagogue and withdrew from them. At this point he apparently rented a commercial assembly hall or lecture hall which belonged to a man named Tyrannus (the regular lecturer or teacher?) and was also being used as a school (Acts 19:9).

Two historical concerns are raised here. First, we may well ask the money came from to rent this hall. It could have been furnished by Priscilla and Aquila, a wealthy convert, the Christian congregation of Ephesus, or Paul may by this time have obtained some personal funds either from offerings, from an inheritance, or from his work as a tentmaker (Acts 20:33-34).

The second historical issue raises the question as to how Paul could be using a hall which was also being used as a school. One ancient text of the book of Acts records that Paul led worship services and held discussions there "from the fifth hour to the tenth" each day, Roman time, that is, from 11:00 a.m. to 4:00 p.m.[2] The choice of these hours was probably due to the fact that this was the time when businesses were generally closed for the midday meal and rest. Thus the school itself would also most likely have been shut down during this time and therefore the building would have been available for a dual use. Although the reference to these hours is not given in the best texts, it clearly makes sense from what we know of Ephesian life from other sources. If we assume that Paul also worked in Ephesus as a tentmaker, these hours would also have been those when he himself was free from his labors as well. The normal work day in Ephesus was from sunup until the fifth hour.[3]

Luke reported that Paul's ministry in the hall of Tyrannus lasted for two years (Acts 19:9-10). This would extend the Ephesian ministry into the early part of AD 56. However, here we encounter another problem in understanding and interpretation. Paul himself later reminded the Ephesian elders that he had served among them for "three years" (Acts 20:31). That could easily be a round number and not really represent exactly thirty-six months. But with the ministry which Luke recorded as being only a total of two years and three months, it would have been more logical for Paul to have

---

[2]This particular text is found in the Codex Bezae. See Robertson, *Word Pictures in the New Testament*, vol. 3, "Acts," 315.

[3]Ramsay, *St. Paul the Traveler and the Roman Citizen*, 270-71.

told the elders that he was with them about two years. However, the fact that Luke reported both statements shows that he apparently saw no conflict between the two.

To deal with this problem, some interpreters suggest that Paul spent some time in prison in Ephesus. This would have been included in the "three years" but would have followed after the three months in the synagogue and the two years in Tyrannus's hall. It seems inconceivable that Luke, who recorded so many of Paul's difficulties during his missionary labors should have omitted any mention of such an eventuality. Possibly supporting the idea of an Ephesian imprisonment is Paul's own statement to the Corinthians that he had suffered "far more imprisonments" than the other apostles (2 Cor. 11:23). However, that seems to be too tenuous a reference upon which to build such a case.

Another possibility, however, suggests itself. As we shall note later in this chapter, Paul experienced major problems with the church at Corinth during his Ephesian ministry. He apparently wrote at least three letters to them during this time and sent Timothy on at least one journey to try to help them. He also seems to have made a hurried journey to Corinth himself during this time. (1 Cor. 16:10; 2 Cor. 1:15; 2:1, 12-13; 13:1). This being the case, perhaps he made his journey to Corinth in Macedonia after the two years in Tyrannus's hall. If so, he would at that point have given up his rental. However, upon his return from Corinth to Ephesus Paul apparently picked up and carried on his Ephesian ministry in some other location.

Although this may not be the proper reconstruction of Paul's time in Ephesus, some such theory must be proposed to solve the chronological problems. This theory at least has an actual basis in Paul's own writings.

In any case, Paul's ministry in Ephesus appears to have extended from late AD 53 to late AD 56. At that point, he decided he needed to visit the churches of Macedonia and Achaia, and then return to Jerusalem. This visit would have been necessitated by the problems with the Corinthian congregation accompanied by his normal desire to see the people in the churches that he had started in that region. However, being the seasoned traveler that he was, Paul would once again certainly not have traveled across the Aegean during the season of winter storms. What, then, would he have done at that point?

Logically, Paul could have continued his ministry in Ephesus, waiting for the start of the spring sailing season. However, it seems that it was at about this time, late AD 56 or early AD 57, that a riot broke out in Ephesus, led by Demetrius the silversmith (Acts 19:23-41). Although the riot eventually was quelled and Paul and his companions escaped unharmed, it was clearly no longer safe for him to remain there. Luke tells us that he "departed for Macedonia" (Acts 20:1). Yet it was still too early for sailing. What did he do? We need to remind ourselves that up the coast of Asia to the north of Ephesus was Troas. Paul had been there before. In fact, he was there when he received his "Macedonian call." He may have even started a church while he was there. What more logical place was there for him to go while waiting for the time when he could once again go over to Macedonia?

Paul apparently had sent word to Titus in Corinth to meet him when he could, perhaps by returning overland. He himself left Ephesus for Troas where he found "a door was opened" for the preaching of the Gospel (2 Cor. 2:12-13). However, as the winter passed away and Titus still had not joined him, his concerns for both Titus and the Corinthian congregation grew. Becoming more and more impatient, Paul finally left his ministry in Troas and "went on to Macedonia" himself. However, when Paul arrived in Macedonia, probably at Philippi, since he seems to have been retracing the steps of his earlier mission, Titus met him, bringing good news about the situation in the congregation at Corinth (2 Cor. 7:5-7, 13). His reunion with Titus, coupled with the fact that his mind and heart were now at ease about the Corinthian church, allowed Paul to spend some time with the churches he had earlier established in that region. Our best estimate is that he spent the spring and summer among the churches of Macedonia, slowly journeying southward. Thus, most likely he would finally have arrived at Corinth in late AD 57.

Ministry in Ephesus and Beyond. Having established a probable chronology for the Ephesian ministry, let us now go back and examine that ministry in a bit more detail. Upon Paul's arrival in Ephesus, he was immediately confronted with some disciples who had neither received Christian baptism nor the gift of the Holy Spirit (Acts 19:1-7). Although the details of this episode are not wholly clear, Paul did insist upon all converts being properly baptized. Further, he clearly did not view the gift of the Spirit as some separate event in a believer's life but as something that should and did accompany Christian baptism. It is interesting to note the apparent difference between the way Paul dealt with these converts and the way Priscilla and Aquila had dealt with Apollos. It is possible that this difference may have been a part of the reason behind some of the problems which arose from the latter's ministry in Corinth.

In Ephesus, as we have seen, Paul ministered to both Jews and Gentiles, following his normal strategy. Although he was not ultimately accepted by the Jews of Ephesus, they were not the ones who created the major opposition for him there. Instead, this came from a silversmith named Demetrius. Demetrius was a pagan and a Gentile, and was supported in his opposition by his fellow silversmiths in Ephesus.[4]

As a result of Paul's labors in the city of Ephesus, the sale of silver shrines dedicated to the goddess Artemis (Diana) fell off as Christian converts and those whom they may have influenced stopped participating in the pagan worship. Thus Demetrius and his fellow silversmiths had suddenly been hit in their purses by Paul's ministry. While they had earlier been unaffected by Paul's preaching, they were quickly aroused when their income fell off. A riot was started by Demetrius which almost turned into a lynching. A mark of Paul's boldness as well as of his sense of self-sacrifice can be seen in the fact that he could hardly be restrained by his disciples from rushing headlong into the center of the riot.

The town clerk finally quelled the uproar by reminding the people that their charges were in error. Paul and his followers had not blasphemed Artemis. He also pointed out that Roman courts existed in which Demetrius might get a redress of his grievances, if he and his fellow craftsmen deserved it.

The theater of Ephesus in which the riot took place could seat about 25,000 people and apparently was filled, or almost so. The Ephesian riot was apparently the largest riot that Paul's preaching had ever produced.[5]

Ephesus was also a center of occult practices and of magic arts. Against that background we must note that Paul's ministry was reported to have been accompanied by several miracles. Unfortunately, these were interpreted by numerous Ephesians as just more of the magic with which they were familiar. However, when some of the magicians tried to imitate Paul's acts, they were defeated and embarrassed. The end result was twofold. First,

---

[4]A good discussion concerning the problems involved in understanding the situation which Paul actually found among these disciples and how he dealt with them is found in Robertson, *Word Pictures in the New Testament*, vol. 3, "Acts," 311-13.

[5]An excellent description of Ephesus accompanied by quality pictures and drawings can be found in Charles F. Pfeiffer and Howard F. Vos, *The Wycliffe Historical Geography of Bible Lands* (Chicago: Moody Press, 1967) 357-65. Note that some writers give the capacity of the theater as 2,400 persons. Someone apparently lost a zero in printing and others have followed this misprint.

the name of Jesus was magnified in the city (Acts 19:17). Second, some among the new Christians had still been practicing their occult arts and at this time they were moved to cut all such ties to their past lives and to burn their scrolls which were related to sorcery.

Paul's ministry in Ephesus was extended into other cities in the province of Asia by his companions. Epaphras apparently was sent to plant churches in Colossae, Laodicea, and Hierapolis (Col. 4:12-13). All seven of the churches addressed in the book of Revelation possibly had their origin in the work of some of Paul's fellow workers at this time (Rev. 2:1, 8, 12, 18; 3:1, 7, 14). During this same time Timothy, Titus, and Erastus ministered in Corinth and perhaps also among the churches of Macedonia (Acts 19:22). Finally, if 1 Timothy is a genuine Pauline epistle, then Timothy had come back from Corinth, joining Paul in Ephesus. At least we know that he was left behind there when Paul departed to go to Macedonia (1 Tim. 1:3).

Paul's mission in Ephesus lasted longer than that in any other city he had visited. That fact by itself probably indicates just how important a center Paul considered it to be. By the time he departed from Ephesus in early AD 57, he had spent a fourth of all the time he had invested in the mission activities recorded by Luke in that one place.

Ultimately, three things seem to have led Paul away from Ephesus. First, the riot of the silversmiths had forced him to see the danger, both for himself and for the church there, of continuing on there for a longer period. Second, the city of Rome was still beckoning him, calling him to the center of the empire (Acts 19:21). Paul the Christian and the Roman citizen would not and could not be content until he had taken the message of his second citizenship to the capital of the first. Third, his ongoing problems with the Corinthian church had made him increasingly eager to see them face to face once again for an extended ministry. And so he left Ephesus. When he did depart, however, the church in Ephesus was firmly established and its influence was felt throughout the region.

The Writings from Ephesus

As we have noted, while Paul was in Ephesus, the church he had established in Corinth had been experiencing a number of major difficulties. First, the congregation had divided into varying factions, each claiming allegiance to one of the great preachers of the day: Peter, Apollos, or Paul. In addition, some of the people with an overbearing piety claimed to follow only Christ, but did nothing to heal the divisions which were developing

(1 Cor. 1:11-12). Second, beyond these divisions within the church, the Christians of Corinth were also putting up with gross immorality on the part of some of its members (1 Cor. 5:1-2). Third, numerous differences of opinion on issues of faith and practice were tearing ever more asunder the fabric of their fellowship. The church was not simply split; it was fragmented.

Paul had apparently first received word of the Corinthian problems directly from the church, followed shortly thereafter by a visit of the servants of Chloe, clearly a close friend of his (1 Cor 1:11). Thoroughly distressed by the news of the church's avalanche of problems, Paul wrote a letter to try to bring some peace into the life of that disturbed congregation. We do not have the text of that letter, although we do have a reference to it from another of Paul's letters (1 Cor. 5:9-11).

Although Paul's first letter to the Christians in Corinth apparently has been lost, we can safely conclude that it failed to achieve the purpose that Paul intended. In fact, it may even have further divided the church, as those who were claiming to follow others even began to question Paul's authority to give commandments or even make suggestions to them in the first place. Paul then wrote a second time, probably dealing with much the same issues all over again. However, in this second letter he was careful to define the basis and nature of his apostolic authority. In addition to sending these two letters, Paul also sent Timothy to Corinth in an attempt to help them sort out and solve their difficulties. It is unclear as to whether Timothy carried the second letter or preceded it. The second letter to the church at Corinth is the one we have in the New Testament as 1 Corinthians.

Apparently Timothy's mission to Corinth was also less than successful, so sometime thereafter Paul himself seems to have made a hurried trip to Corinth from Ephesus, as discussed above. This seems likely based on the fact that Paul later wrote the Corinthians, promising a third visit (2 Cor. 13:1). For Paul to plan a "third" visit, a second visit has to have occurred somewhere during this time. However, like the visit of Timothy, Paul's visit also apparently failed to bring a peaceful solution to the Corinthian problems. So Paul had returned to Ephesus in heartache and bitterness. We have no way of really dating this second visit, but it seems to fit best into the period immediately following his two-year rental of the hall of Tyrannus. If this is correct, Paul's hurried visit from Ephesus to Corinth would have been in early AD 56.

Upon Paul's return from Corinth to Ephesus in spiritual defeat, he wrote a third letter to the disturbed and disturbing congregation at Corinth. This has been identified by Pauline interpreters with the title of "the harsh letter." It was a letter which Paul claimed to have truly regretted having to write (2 Cor. 7:8-12). Here again we have a reference to a letter of which we no longer have a copy.[6] Paul seems to have sent Titus to deliver that letter and to return with the Corinthians' response.

Apparently, shortly thereafter the Ephesian riot occurred and Paul decided to leave Ephesus, beginning one more journey to Macedonia and Achaia by way of Troas. Given his obvious anxiety over the Corinthian situation, the only possible reason major enough to keep him from sailing directly across the Aegean to Corinth was the fact that it was winter. It appears most likely therefore that his departure from Ephesus should be dated in late AD 56 or early AD 57.

While in Ephesus, Paul experienced some kind of "affliction" (2 Cor. 1:8-11). His condition apparently seemed to be quite serious, even to the point of being life threatening. This has been variously interpreted by some as being some sort of illness, while others consider it to have been an imprisonment. The former appears to be more likely than the latter. However, since the only reference to it is found in the Corinthian correspondence, it is at least likely that this "affliction" was his heartache and depression at what was happening to and in the Corinthian church, as well as the disruption of fellowship between them and him.

Paul moved north along the coast from Ephesus to Troas, arriving there for the second time. Paul seemingly had a successful ministry during his stay there while awaiting an opportunity to go on toward Macedonia and Achaia. However, he was still deeply troubled by the problems with the Corinthian church. This anxiety left him very impatient, an impatience which was only augmented by Titus's failure to join him in Troas bringing a report of his visit with the disturbed church (2 Cor. 2:12-13). Therefore, even though his ministry at Troas was meeting with success, as soon as was safely possible Paul left Troas and proceeded onward to Macedonia, with his ultimate destination being Corinth. However, while he was on the way, Titus finally rejoined him, probably at Philippi, bearing good news about the situation in Corinth.

Upon receiving the report of Titus that the Corinthians' troubles had been successfully settled, Paul wrote a fourth letter to the church in Corinth

---

[6]Some commentators have suggested that a fragment of that third letter has been appended to what we know as 2 Corinthians 1–9, that is, as chapters 10–13.

(2 Cor 7:5-6, 13). Because of Titus's good news, Paul at this time wrote a very joyous letter. This letter is preserved in the New Testament as 2 Corinthians.[7]

The Mission in Macedonia and Achaia

With the Corinthian problem apparently solved, Paul was no longer in such a hurry to get to Corinth. This left him free to spend some time visiting the churches in Macedonia that he had established on his earlier mission there. As we noted earlier, he, along with Titus and possibly Timothy, seems finally to have arrived in Corinth late in AD 57. He remained there for about three months, ministering and renewing friendships (Acts 20:3). This would have brought him into the early months of AD 58. During this time he wrote his letter to the church at Rome, expressing his desire and intent to come to them eventually (Rom. 1:11-15).

Apparently Paul had planned to leave Corinth in the spring, catching the earliest ship sailing for Judea in order to be back in Jerusalem for Passover. At such a time a large group of Jewish pilgrims from the Diaspora of Achaia would have been making their way to Jerusalem for that feast. Unfortunately, some of Paul's enemies were also among them, plotting to kill him along the way. Judging from the way he dealt with this plot, their plan apparently had been to throw him overboard once the ship had reached the deep sea.

In order to thwart their plot, Paul sent his companions onto the ship, having instructed them to wait for him at Troas, apparently the first landfall scheduled for the vessel. In the meantime he, accompanied by some friends serving as a bodyguard in the event of a land-based attack, went overland to Philippi and its port city, Neapolis. This journey slowed down his travel plans and so he celebrated Passover and the Feast of Unleavened Bread, the two great Jewish festivals, in Philippi. Following that, he sailed for Troas to rejoin his friends who, having sailed earlier from Corinth, were awaiting him there (Acts 20:5-6).

After a brief visit at Troas, Paul and his companions started the voyage onward to Jerusalem. For the first part of their journey, they obviously had taken a coastal vessel which halted each evening. By necessity, Paul had changed his schedule, now hoping to be in Jerusalem for Pentecost, the

---

[7]The joyous part of 2 Corinthians is chapters 1–9. We have already noted that some interpreters believe that chapters 10–13 are a fragment of the earlier "harsh letter."

feast fifty days after Passover. As they proceeded along the way, he met with the elders of the Ephesian church at the port of Miletus, bidding them goodbye. Both he and they knew that Paul's increasing age coupled with his desire to minister in Rome made it likely that these beloved friends would almost certainly never meet again (Acts 20:36-38). From Miletus, he and his companions continued to sail on coastal ships until they came to Patara, where they picked up a deep-sea vessel bound for Tyre and Caesarea (Acts 21:1-6).

On the last leg of this journey, Luke carefully noted that the ship they were on passed by Cyprus. We can only imagine what thoughts went through Paul's mind at that time. Cyprus was the only site where Paul had ministered and started churches to which he had never returned, at least insofar as is recorded in Acts. That was probably due to his angry separation from Barnabas, for at that time his old friend and John Mark had returned to Cyprus (Acts 15:39). The old wound of that angry parting must have burned deeply. We can only wonder if by this time the great apostle had any feelings of sorrow, regret, remorse, or forgiveness.

When their ship arrived at Tyre, Paul and his companions spent a brief time with the Christians there while the ship off-loaded cargo. We have no record of Paul having ministered before at Tyre. However, given its location and what we have been able to reconstruct of Paul's so-called "silent years," he may possibly have even started the congregation there. Knowing the situation in Jerusalem better than Paul at that time, the members warned him not to go on. That city, always turbulent at the occasion of the major festivals, was especially so at that moment. However, the Spirit thrust him onward, so when the ship was ready to sail for Caesarea, Paul and his companions boarded for the final leg of their voyage.

Shortly thereafter, Paul and those with him finally reached Caesarea. Once again he was warned not to go on to Jerusalem. This time the warning was given by a prophet performing a typical symbolic act, binding his own feet and hands with the belt which Paul had around his waist.[8] Paul, however, was still not to be deterred. Jerusalem was his planned destination and Jerusalem was where he would go, regardless of the personal cost. So it was that, in spite of all the warnings, they departed from there and "went up to Jerusalem" (Acts 21:8-15).

---

[8]A brief discussion of the symbolic acts of the prophets can be found in my *Old Testament Roots for New Testament Faith* (Nashville: Broadman Press, 1982) 41.

Just before Pentecost in the early summer of AD 58, therefore, Paul arrived at the Holy City for his final visit. He was about to make the last free move he might ever make. For Paul, Jerusalem was where this amazing pilgrimage had all begun, as he had led out in the persecution of the Christians. In Jerusalem it would begin to come to an end, with him being the one upon whom the whole frustrated fury of the Sanhedrin toward Christianity would be unleashed. Only his Roman citizenship spared him a similar fate in Jerusalem from that which was experienced by his Lord. His utter commitment, his steadfast faith, and his sense of God's hand upon him led him to say with utmost simplicity, "I am ready not only to be imprisoned but even to die in Jerusalem for the name of the Lord Jesus" (Acts 21:13).

Chapter 7

From Jerusalem to Rome

In Luke's Gospel, the Beloved Physician carefully recorded Jesus' words as he looked toward the end of his life: "I must go on my way today and tomorrow and the day following; for it cannot be that a prophet should perish away from Jerusalem" (Luke 13:33). With that as a foundation, Luke then appears to have quite carefully built the latter half of his Gospel around the deliberate movement of Jesus toward the place and time of his death, beginning with the words, "He set his face to go to Jerusalem" (Luke 9:51). From that time forward in Luke's record of the Gospel, nothing enters into his narrative that does not bring Jesus closer to the cross.[1]

In precisely the same way, Luke seems to have built the story of Paul's final years around that apostle's deliberate movement toward Rome by way of Jerusalem. In this narrative, he recorded the same purposeful determination on the part of Paul which began in Corinth near the end of the third missionary journey, simply pointing out that "he was about to set sail for Syria," where Jerusalem was located (Acts 20:3). From that moment on, everything in the narrative reveals the determination of the Apostle Extraordinary to achieve this goal. Nothing was allowed to sway him from his predetermined purpose. Neither a threat on his life in Corinth, the tears of his friends in Ephesus, the pleas of the disciples in Tyre, the warning of Agabus at Caesarea, nor the insistence of his companions along the way, dissuaded Paul from his obvious purpose or turned him aside on his journey. Note how Luke developed this theme.

> [W]hen a plot was made against him . . . [Paul] determined to return through Macedonia. (Acts 20:3)
>
> [W]e sailed away from Philippi after the days of Unleavened Bread, and in five days we came to . . . Troas, where we stayed for seven days. (Acts 20:6)
>
> Paul talked with them, intending to depart on the morrow. (Acts 20:7)
>
> [W]e set sail for Assos, intending to take Paul aboard there; for so he had arranged. (Acts 20:13)
>
> [W]hen he met us at Assos, we took him on board and came to Mitylene. (Acts 20:14)
>
> We came the following day opposite Chios; the next day we touched at Samos; and the day after that we came to Miletus. (Acts 20:15)

---

[1]A brief treatment of Luke's development of this theme can be seen in Cate, *A History of the New Testament and Its Times*, 173-74.

Paul had determined to sail past Ephesus, . . . for he was hastening to be at Jerusalem . . . on the day of Pentecost. (Acts 20:16)

[T]he Holy Spirit testifies to me in every city that imprisonment and afflictions await me. (Acts 20:23)

[T]hey . . . wept . . . , sorrowing most of all . . . that they should see his face no more. And they brought him to the ship. (Acts 20:37-38)

[W]e . . . set sail . . . by a straight course to Cos, and the next day to Rhodes, and from there to Patara. (Acts 21:1)

[H]aving found a ship crossing to Phoenicia, we . . . set sail. (Acts 21:2)

[W]e . . . [came] in sight of Cyprus, . . . we sailed to Syria, and landed at Tyre. (Acts 21:3)

[T]hey told Paul not to go on to Jerusalem. (Acts 21:4)

[W]e departed and went on our journey. (Acts 21:5)

[W]e went on board the ship. (Acts 21:6)

[W]e . . . finished the voyage from Tyre, we arrived at Ptolemais. (Acts 21:7)

On the morrow we departed and came to Caesarea. (Acts 21:8)

Agabus . . . took Paul's girdle and bound his own feet and hands, and said, . . . "So shall the Jews at Jerusalem bind the man who owns this girdle and deliver him into the hands of the Gentiles." (Acts 21:10-11)

[W]e and the people . . . begged him not to go up to Jerusalem. (Acts 21:12)

[H]e would not be persuaded. (Acts 21:14)

[W]e made ready and went up to Jerusalem. (Acts 21:15)

[We came] to Jerusalem. (Acts 21:17)

Paul's words and deeds throughout this entire process clearly reveal that he knew that the end of both ministry and life was approaching with studied speed. Like the beat of a drum increasing both in tempo and volume, the days of Paul's ministry were rapidly but deliberately drawing to a close. He assured his friends that he was ready either to be imprisoned or to die at Jerusalem (Acts 21:13). He was imprisoned there, but his death was delayed at least until he reached his ultimate goal of Rome. Sadly, he arrived at Rome as a prisoner rather than as a missionary as he had planned.

Paul's opponents, like those of his Lord, had tried over and over again to kill him during the dramatic days of his ministry. But also like his Lord, it almost seems as if it were Paul who determined both the time and place of his arrest and death rather than they. Paul's last days were, if anything, more dramatic and more filled with his missionary passion than any which had passed before. This is the story of their passage.

Arrest and Imprisonment

Assuming that our chronological reconstruction to this point has been correct, Paul seems to have arrived in Jerusalem just before Pentecost in June AD 58. We know that this was the season of the year for which he had been striving (Acts 20:16). Although Luke does not actually say that Paul made it by that time, most likely the failure would have been reported if he hadn't. Furthermore, the fact that there were a large number of "Jews from Asia" in the Temple when Paul visited it would most likely indicate that some great festival was being celebrated which would have brought in pilgrims from the Diaspora. No festival other than Pentecost would fit the situation (Acts 21:27).

When Paul arrived in Jerusalem, he went immediately to meet with James and the elders of the church, according to his custom (Acts 21:18-26). Throughout his entire life, Paul had shown himself to be a person of disciplined habits. He stuck with normal patterns for living, allowing them to serve as guides for his behavior.

Several features of that meeting stand out as significant. First, James, Jesus' brother, was still the official leader of the church. Second, not one of the apostles is mentioned. It is likely that some of them had already died while others may have been away on preaching missions. However, the important fact is that the Jerusalem church was now able to function well without their leadership or even their presence. It had clearly matured.

The third feature of that meeting in Jerusalem which is significant for our study is that Luke did not even bother to mention the offering which Paul had gathered from his churches and which was surely delivered at this point (1 Cor. 16:1-4). Although such an offering had to have been quite significant for the Jerusalem church, it was obviously not the primary concern of either Paul or the church leaders. It certainly wasn't Luke's primary concern.

Fourth, when Paul reported on the successes of his missionary endeavors, although the Jerusalem leaders rejoiced, they did not dwell on these for they had other concerns on their minds at the moment, concerns which to them were far more important.

This brings us to the fifth and major feature of the meeting between Paul and the Jerusalem church leaders, and this was Paul's reputation among some of the people of Jerusalem, including both the Jewish Christians and the Jews themselves, especially the Sanhedrin. Regardless of new developments, the Sanhedrin particularly still smarted from what they perceived as Paul's earlier betrayal. Added to those old wounds, however, word had been brought back to Jerusalem from the mission fields where Paul had labored that he had been leading Jewish Christians in his churches to forsake Judaism (Acts 21:21). This was simply not true. Certainly Paul had not required Gentiles to become Jews and he had consistently pointed out the fact that the Law was unable to save, but he himself had remained a practicing Jew and had led no one else to do otherwise. The very fact that he had at first wished to be in Jerusalem for the Passover and then had striven so hard to arrive by Pentecost were clear indications of his ongoing commitment to Judaism for himself.

James and the elders of the Jerusalem church, however, were desperately afraid that Paul's presence in Jerusalem would be an affront both to the Jews and to the Jewish Christians there. Because of their fear, the church leaders had already thought about this problem, having probably begun when they had first received word that Paul was on his way. Thus they already had a proposal ready to suggest to Paul when he arrived which they hoped would ease the situation.

In those days, when people had made a Nazirite vow and reached the time of its completion, they were required to shave their head and to offer the proper sacrifices. This included two lambs and one ram and was accompanied by the proper meal and drink offerings (Num. 6:1-15).[2] A poor person could not furnish such extravagant offerings. Thus it had become the custom for such people to wait at the Temple gates, or at least near the Temple precincts in Jerusalem, for some more wealthy person who would furnish the offerings as an act of both charity and piety.

The Jerusalem church leaders suggested that Paul should furnish these offerings for four of the poorer Nazirites of Jerusalem (Acts 21:23-24). It is possible that these men may even have been part of the Jerusalem church. Further, since he himself had earlier fulfilled such a vow, it is possible that he may even have been doing it again (Acts 18:18). In presenting their case to Paul, the Jerusalem elders reminded him of the earlier decree of the council: that while Gentiles did not have to become Jews, Jews were expected to remain so. Paul agreed with their suggestion and set out to follow it. Unfortunately, all of them were wrong in their assessment of the

---

[2]The nature of the Nazirite vow and the processes of bringing it to an end are discussed in Robertson, *Word Pictures in the New Testament*, vol. 3, "Acts," 369-73; and in Ramsay, *St. Paul the Traveler and the Roman Citizen*, 310. The Talmud also discusses the issue.

situation. Conditions in Jerusalem were far more volatile than any among them had imagined.

The hatred and jealousy that was directed toward Paul was so intense that the confrontation was not to be avoided by such a subtle and indirect act. In fact, it was not to be avoided by any means. When Paul was recognized in the Temple by some Jews from Asia, a riot broke out. The Asian Jews made two false charges against Paul. First, they charged him with leading people away from Judaism. Much more serious at the moment, however, they charged him with having brought "Greeks into the temple" (Acts 21:28). This was a crime that was punishable by death.

Word of the riot was quickly reported to the Roman tribune who commanded the cohort stationed in Jerusalem at major feast days, prepared for just such outbreaks. Roman troops were stationed at such times in the tower of Antonia, immediately adjacent to the Temple precincts. Rushing to the scene, the troops seized Paul while their commander sought to find out who he was and what he had done. Getting many answers and seeing that the riot was about to break out again, he ordered Paul to be carried into the barracks for Paul's own protection and for further investigation (Acts 21:30-36). Note that at this moment, the Roman invaders were placed in the almost humorous position of protecting Paul from his own people. This became the pattern throughout all of the subsequent events.

As the Roman soldiers sought to bring Paul through the mob into the safety of the Antonia, he managed to speak to the commander, using the Greek language. At that, the tribune was startled, for he had assumed that Paul was an Egyptian rabble-rouser who, as Josephus had recorded, had earlier caused the Romans some major trouble. Quickly recognizing his misidentification, the officer granted Paul's request, permitting him to address the crowd, perhaps hoping to gain some information about what had started the riot in the first place. Paul then began to speak to the crowd in Aramaic, their own language (Acts 21:37-40). They listened briefly as he told of his commitment to Judaism and his conversion to Christianity. However, when he told of his "call" to go to the Gentiles, the riot broke out all over again (Acts 22:1-23).

At that point, the Roman commander had had enough. He ordered Paul to be carried into the fortress, where he was to be interrogated by scourging. While this was both a legal as well as a normal procedure, it was not supposed to be carried out against a Roman citizen. Paul, overhearing what was about to be done to him, appealed to his Roman citizenship. Both shocked and frightened by this bit of information, the tribune ordered his soldiers to release Paul from most of his bindings (Acts 22:24-29). Roman citizens could be bound only by the hands if they had not been convicted of a crime.

Still trying to find out what Paul had done to arouse such a reaction from the people of Jerusalem, the next day the tribune took him before the Sanhedrin. Apparently the tribune could not speak Aramaic, or he would have understood those events better after the second riot had broken out. After a brief confrontation with one of the more unscrupulous men ever to be high priest (Ananias), Paul finally spoke to the whole body. Realizing that most of the members of the high court were either Pharisees or Sadducees, Paul created a division among them by talking about the resurrection, a subject about which the two parties disagreed vehemently. Paul's words had the intended effect, causing a major dissension among the Sanhedrin itself. Once again, fearing for the safety of his prisoner, the Romans whisked Paul away from the turmoil and back to their barracks (Acts 23:1-11).

Following this development, a group of about forty Jewish "terrorists" took an oath to kill Paul. The Sanhedrin, to their discredit, due to their continuing hostility toward Paul, entered into the plot. They were to request that the Romans would once again bring Paul before them, ostensibly for another hearing. However, the intent was that the terrorists would assassinate him along the way. The number of assassins were clearly thought to be sufficient to take Paul away from his Roman guards by the surprise and violence of their attack (Acts 23:12-15).

This treacherous project was thwarted, however, by an unusual development that took place at this point. Paul's nephew, his sister's son, found out about the plot (Acts 23:16). What surprises us here is that, prior to this, no member of Paul's family has been mentioned, either in Luke's narrative or in any of Paul's epistles. Paul's sister was apparently living in Jerusalem. It seems unlikely that she was a Christian, or we would expect that she would have been mentioned somewhere among all of Paul's comings and goings there. Furthermore, the plotters surely would not have allowed any of Paul's Christian friends to learn about their plan.

Paul's nephew—and presumably his sister—must have been a trusted member of the anti-Christian Jews in Jerusalem or a close associate of someone who was. Possibly the nephew or his father was actually a member of the Sanhedrin. Given Paul's original associations with both the high priest and Gamaliel, as well as with the other members of the Sanhedrin, it is possible that his sister and her son were also friends of one or more of these. In any case, when Paul's nephew found out about the plot, he felt duty bound to warn Paul of the treachery plotted against him. Family ties were always important to the Jewish people.

When Paul heard of this new threat to his life, he sent his nephew to tell the Roman tribune about it. Realizing that the situation surrounding Paul was about to get totally out of hand, the tribune immediately made plans to send Paul to the governor in the provincial capital, Caesarea. He seems to have felt that at least there the apostle could be imprisoned in safety. Further, this would then give the Roman procurator, Felix, time to investigate and, if necessary, try Paul. So seriously did the tribune take the threat that he sent Paul out of Jerusalem with a unit of seventy horsemen and two hundred spearmen, ordering them to depart under cover of darkness (Acts 23:23-24).

This troop movement escorting Paul accomplished three purposes. First, the soldiers were of sufficient number to protect Paul from any terrorists' attack. Second, sending troops out of Jerusalem at night during a festal season was not unusual, as the Romans normally tried not to antagonize unduly the pilgrims who thronged the city at such times. Thus it would not particularly have attracted the attention of Paul's enemies. Third, sending such a large number of soldiers would have made it appear to any watchers that they were going on some kind of military mission. They certainly would not have appeared to be furnishing protection for just one prisoner. In any case, the stratagem was successful and Paul arrived safely in Caesarea (Acts 23:31-33).

The Imprisonment at Caesarea

At the time it began, no one would ever have thought that Paul's imprisonment at Caesarea would have dragged on for two years. Shortly after Paul's arrival from Jerusalem, he had a hearing before the Roman procurator, Felix. There representatives of the Sanhedrin presented their case before the governor and Paul was allowed to respond. The immediate result of this confrontation was that Felix postponed making a decision, awaiting the report of the events which was to be submitted by his tribune, Lysias (Acts 24:22).

Several other features of Paul's incarceration call for consideration at this point, however. With the initial hearing being held in the summer of AD 58, Felix had been serving as procurator for six years. During this time he had learned a great deal both about the Jewish people whom he governed and also about "the Way" of which Paul was a part. Felix was possibly hoping that by postponing a decision, the attention of the Sanhedrin would soon be directed to some other issue and the whole matter would be dropped. If this were the case, Felix seriously underestimated the Sanhedrin's hatred of Paul. Felix also appears to have had a more ulterior motive for delaying his decision, for he hoped that somewhere along the way Paul or his friends might bribe the governor to release the prisoner from Tarsus.

At this point, we become aware of what appears to be a new dimension in Paul's life. Although he had labored as a tentmaker to support himself on his missionary journeys, Paul was apparently by this time a person of some significant financial resources. This impression seems to have been received by all those who came to know him during this period. Lest there be some question of this conclusion, Paul's direct actions also appear to confirm this. The ability to have gone to Jerusalem as a youth to study to become a rabbi probably indicated that at that time his father possessed significant financial resources. Even more, the fact that Paul's sister and her son were now in Jerusalem and moving freely among the Jewish leaders may also reveal the same thing.

In addition, the fact that the Jerusalem church leaders and Paul all assumed that he could afford to pay for the sacrifices of four impoverished Nazirites indicates the resources that he had available.[3] However, perhaps of even more importance, the fact that Paul was imprisoned in Felix's palace rather than in the customary prison indicates the governor's estimate of his prisoner's importance. In addition, the fact that Felix took the occasion of Paul's imprisonment to converse with him regularly reveals the same thing. Governors past or present simply do not entertain or waste time with impoverished prisoners.

Furthermore, when Paul finally appealed his case to Caesar's tribunal, that whole process revealed significant financial resources on his part. The journey to Rome had to be made at Paul's own expense. Those who appealed their cases in such a manner were required to bear the expenses of

---

[3]Some have suggested that the church there might have given funds to Paul to accomplish this. This is unlikely, since the Jerusalem church's financial situation was such that Paul had actually brought a relief offering from the Macedonian churches with him. Others suggest that funds from the relief offering were given by the elders to Paul for this purpose. Again, it is unlikely they would have made such an offering from funds desperately needed for other purposes and even more unlikely that Paul would have taken such funds for his own use. This is discussed in Robertson, *Word Pictures in the New Testament*, vol. 3, "Acts"; and in Ramsay, *St. Paul the Traveler and the Roman Citizen*, 310-12.

such an appeal. Finally, when Paul finally arrived in Rome, his ability to hire a house where he lived for two years under house arrest while awaiting his trial also indicates some measure of financial resources. It is highly possible that somewhere along the way Paul had inherited a significant estate from his father. Admittedly, it is also possible that all of Paul's resources at this time came from the contributions of his friends. However, while Paul had accepted such gifts in the past, it was always for the purpose of allowing him to carry on his ministry. It seems to be unlikely that he would have accepted sacrificially given funds sufficient to have covered what all this would have cost just to meet his own personal needs.

Additionally, all the events surrounding Paul's arrest in Jerusalem and his imprisonment in Caesarea raise the issue of the total silence throughout this time of the Christians from the Jerusalem church. We have no record of them doing anything either to rescue or even to help him while he was in Jerusalem. Neither is there any record of their aid or even of their communication of comfort after he had been carried to Caesarea. We know that the church in Jerusalem had been bold at other times. We must ask why there is no record of any bold action on their part during this entire episode of Paul's critical need. Admittedly, Luke may have left out such references as not being germane to what he was trying to communicate. At the same time, a two-year imprisonment with no evidence that the Christians of Jerusalem even visited Paul makes it highly suggestive that, on their part, there was little love lost for Paul.

Admittedly, Paul had been a great missionary. Yet, as is frequently the case with such active, aggressive people, he was constantly creating problems for those around him. This was especially true for the Jerusalem congregation and particularly so for their leaders. At the very least, as we read this material and note what is *not* said, we are left with a feeling of sadness that apparently Paul was left without any significant aid or expression of concern from the church at Jerusalem, a congregation with which he had obviously felt strong ties.

At the same time, Paul's bold confrontation of Felix and his wife Drusilla is almost unbelievable. Paul's words about justice must have stirred memories of the many injustices that history records of Felix. His words about self-control surely brought to the minds of both the governor and his wife the unbridled lust which had led to their marriage in the first place. And Paul's words about future judgment just as surely must have struck fear in their hearts. Yet, in spite of all this, Paul was allowed great freedom by the governor and was frequently called into his presence for additional conversations (Acts 24:24-27).

In AD 60, two years after Paul was first imprisoned, a violent confrontation occurred between Gentiles and Jews in Caesarea. Felix was so fed up with such events that he allowed his troops to kill numerous Jews in quelling the riot as well as allowing them to loot Jewish homes. When this was reported to Rome by the Jewish leaders, Felix was immediately removed from office and just barely escaped being executed.[4] Although he had never found any cause for punishing Paul, the departing governor left him in prison in a vain attempt to appease his Jewish opposition. He apparently did not wish to risk making them any more hostile toward him as he departed. His future advancement in the Roman bureaucracy still depended upon their testimony.

In the summer of AD 60, Porcius Festus arrived in Caesarea to replace Felix as procurator. Immediately upon his arrival, the Jewish leaders sought to incite him against Paul. Being new at his post, he apparently knew little or nothing about Christianity or of the Jewish-Christian conflict. But he clearly did know that to have any opportunity of success as governor of Judea, he had to win the favor of the Sanhedrin and do it quickly. Having seen the influential power of their opposition demonstrated in the removal of his predecessor, Festus did not wish to have the Jewish leaders as opponents.

Thus when Festus had Paul brought in for an initial hearing, he suggested to the apostle what made good sense to him, that Paul go to Jerusalem for a hearing before, or at least in the presence of, the Sanhedrin. At this point, Paul seems finally to have realized that his chances of ever finding freedom from the Roman rulers of Palestine were very small. Having become utterly frustrated with provincial Roman justice, he made his appeal to Caesar's tribunal (Acts 25:1-12).

Any Roman citizen had the right to appeal his case to the courts of Caesar in Rome, provided that no judgment had been rendered against him by a provincial court or ruler. We need to recognize that this was not an appeal to a higher court for the purpose of overturning the judgment of a lower one. Rather than being an appeal for a reversal of a prior decision, this was essentially a request for a transfer or change of venue to another jurisdiction. Roman citizens well knew that the cost of any such appeal

---

[4]Cate, *A History of the New Testament and Its Times*, 281.

must always be borne by the accused. The empire was not going to pay for anyone to vacation in Rome.

At that point, Festus had no alternative but to grant Paul's request for a change of venue to Caesar's courts. However, before he could send Paul, he had to draw up a document setting forth the charges against Paul along with a statement of all relevant evidence. While this had to be done as quickly as possible, the task was obviously not high on the list of priorities for a governor assuming his administrative responsibilities in a new assignment.

During this time of delay, Agrippa II and his wife Bernice came to Caesarea, apparently to pay their respects to the new Roman official. Knowing of Agrippa's Jewish background, Festus spoke to his visitor about Paul, apparently seeking help from him in writing the official letter by which he would transfer the case to Rome's jurisdiction. To facilitate the process, Paul was brought before Agrippa to give his defense. However, instead of defending himself, Paul simply told the story of his life, conversion, and ministry as an explanation of why he was in the situation in which he now found himself (Acts 25:23–26:29).

The end result of Paul's hearing before Agrippa was that once again not one thing was found worthy of convicting Paul. Both Agrippa and Festus agreed that Paul had done "nothing to deserve death or imprisonment" (Acts 26:31). However, since the apostle had already appealed his case to Caesar, he had to be sent there. We ought to note that, since Paul had already appealed to Caesar, Festus was free to render a judgment that did not have to be implemented. If there had been no appeal, it seems unlikely that Festus would have released Paul lest he offend the Jewish leaders.

Paul's appeal to Caesar was at long last going to end the farce which had been carried out in Caesarea. Paul was finally going to Rome. However, he was not going there in the manner he had originally intended.

One major feature stands out in Luke's narrative of Paul's arrest and imprisonment. *In not one single instance where Paul had been given a hearing before any Roman official was he ever found guilty*. While not always being declared innocent, he was never declared to be guilty of wrongdoing by Rome or by any of her officials. Throughout the entire narrative, Paul's Christian ministry was never seen by Rome as being illegal, traitorous, seditious, or threatening.

From Caesarea to Rome

By the time Paul finally sailed from Caesarea, it was probably mid- to late September in AD 60. Paul had to have been an old man when judged by the standards of that day, at least sixty years old. He was accompanied on the arduous trip by Aristarchus (identified by name) and also probably by Luke, for the narrative again reverts to a "we-section" (Acts 27:1-2).

The events of the sea voyage are quite detailed in their narration. Further, as has been pointed out earlier, Luke's narrative reflects a very accurate knowledge of the sailing practices and conditions in the Mediterranean at that time in history.

When the ship sailed, the Roman soldiers had in their care other prisoners in addition to Paul. However, Luke's narrative makes it quite plain that Paul was treated differently from the others. Most, if not all, of the others were apparently men who had been convicted of crimes and were being sent to Rome to fight with gladiators or wild animals as part of Nero's entertainment for the masses.

The season was apparently late for sailing when the group set forth, so they took a coastal vessel which would tend to stay close inshore, following the northeastern corner of the Mediterranean (Acts 27:2). The Roman commander's apparent intent was to try to get as far as Neapolis by ship, subsequently marching by the Egnatian Way across Macedonia. From there they would have had a short and protected voyage over a narrow part of the Adriatic to Italy, allowing them to arrive in Rome before the year's end. At least, that would have been a normal route for them to have attempted in order to try to get to Rome both quickly and safely during the season when the winter storms were approaching.

The situation obviously changed, however, when they arrived at the port of Myra. There they found "a ship of Alexandria," bound for Italy. Taking the opportunity when it presented itself, the centurion transferred his troops and his prisoners to that vessel, obviously hoping to arrive in Rome much more quickly than they could possibly have done if they had gone overland through Macedonia (Acts 27:5-6).

In order to understand some of the details of the remainder of the voyage, we need to note what is meant by the expression, "a ship of Alexandria." First, Egypt was the major supplier of grain to Rome at that time. This grain was normally shipped from the major Egyptian port of Alexandria. "Ships of Alexandria" were therefore normally grain ships, supplying

Rome's hearty appetite for bread. They would compare to the ordinary ships of that day as supertankers compare with ordinary freighters of today.

Further, such ships which arrived late in the fall season, since they were bringing grain which had to last over the winter, as well as those which arrived earliest in the spring, since they were bringing fresh grain to replenish Rome's depleted supplies, could expect to receive the highest prices for their cargo. Thus, even though there was obviously a significant risk added to the journey by sailing at the time of the beginning of the winter storms, successful voyages resulted in much larger profits for the grain merchants. That this ship on which Paul sailed was such a ship is confirmed by Luke, for when it was later about to founder, we are told that they then threw out "the wheat into the sea" (Acts 27:38).

Although some contemporary writers have suggested that, to be in Myra, a ship sailing from Alexandria to Rome must already have been blown off course by a major storm. They are mistaken. Given the direction of the prevailing winds at that season of the year, in the first century AD the normal sailing route from Alexandria to Rome crossed the Mediterranean directly to Myra and then turned westward to Rome.[5]

The second piece of information conveyed by the expression, "a ship of Alexandria," is the fact that such a ship was a part of the Roman fleet, not a private merchant ship. With Rome wholly dependent upon this source for the supply of their bread, they would never have dared risk that grain supply to the changing fortunes and wills of men of commerce. In fact, whenever we have such records from contemporary Roman administrations, it is clear that the department of government in charge of furnishing bread to the city of Rome was the most important one of all. Thus "a ship of Alexandria" was a part of the official fleet of Rome. The cargo on such ships was privately owned, but the ship was under the direct control of Rome itself.[6]

That this vessel on which Paul sailed was a Roman ship, not a merchant vessel, makes understandable the fact that, after the Roman centurion went on board the ship, it was he who presided over any council meeting seeking to determine the course to take or the place and time to anchor. Rome, like most ancient governments, did not have a separate army and navy. The

---

[5]Ramsay, *St. Paul the Traveler and the Roman Citizen*, 316-20, provides a good discussion of the normal sailing patterns for ships in the northeastern Mediterranean at this season of the year.

[6]Ramsay, *St. Paul the Traveler and the Roman Citizen*, 323-24.

highest ranking military officer on board was the one in ultimate command
of any Roman ship.

Once again, in the centurion's attitude toward Paul on this journey, we
see further evidence of the apostle's significance and influence. From
contemporary documents of the time, it appears that Roman policy forbade
that any prisoner should be accompanied on such journeys by friends or
family. However, prisoners of wealth and distinction were allowed to be
accompanied by their slaves.[7] Thus Luke and Aristarchus apparently passed
themselves off as Paul's slaves. To have been accompanied by two slaves
on his voyage to Rome would have made Paul appear even more significant
in the eyes of the Roman commander. It is possible that Paul was sick at the
beginning of the voyage, for when they put in briefly at Sidon, the centurion
allowed Paul's friends there to care for him (Acts 27:3) In addition,
whenever conferences were held to make decisions regarding the further
course of the voyage, the Roman commander always seems to have
included Paul. And later, when the ship was about to sink, he followed
Paul's advice to the letter. The centurion clearly believed that Paul was a
man of substance and significance, as well as a person with extensive
nautical experience, one who could be fully trusted. He certainly does not
seem to have acted in that manner toward any of the other prisoners.

As Paul's ship made its way across the Mediterranean, they eventually
came to a small harbor named Fair Havens on the southern coast of Crete.
We are told that they were now well into the dangerous season for sailing,
as "the fast" had already gone by (Acts 27:9). The "fast" was Yom Kippur,
the Jews' great Day of Atonement.[8] Its precise date was regulated by the
lunar calendar and could occur in various years anywhere from mid-Sep-
tember to mid-October. Ship movements in that part of the Mediterranean
were considered to be quite dangerous by mid-October and impossible by
mid-November. Most likely, Paul and his companions were now at mid- to
late October, AD 60. If it had been later than that, Luke would almost certainly have referred to their celebration of the Feast of Tabernacles as well.

Although the soldiers, the prisoners, the passengers, the crew, and their
ship were temporarily secure, the sailors among them pointed out that Fair
Havens was not a suitable port in which to spend the winter, being too open

---

[7]Ramsay, *St. Paul the Traveler and the Roman Citizen*, 315-16.

[8]Luke's simple reference to "the fast" is probably an indication that while Paul and
Aristarchus, as good Jews, had celebrated it, he himself had not. If it had been important to
him, he would certainly have referred to it as *Yom Kippur*, the Day of Atonement.

to the storms which customarily swept in from the Mediterranean. At the same time, however, Paul advised against proceeding onwards. However, the sailors and the owners of the grain wished to get to Phoenix, somewhat farther along their way and possessing a more sheltered harbor, even though it was located on the western coast of Crete (Acts 27:12).

We need to note that the word here translated as "owner" (Acts 27:11) is not the normal word to describe the owner of a ship. As we have already seen, the ship most likely belonged to Rome itself. The word used here, then, must refer to the man who owned the grain. As such he was a businessman looking for the highest profit he could obtain. Since it was now obvious that he could not get his grain to Rome before the winter storms, the next best alternative was to get his grain as close to Rome as possible at that time so he could get his produce to Rome as early as possible in the spring.

Thus the ship finally set sail from Fair Havens when it appeared that they had a fair wind blowing. Unfortunately, a major winter storm was right behind. The ship was soon caught by its wrath and was driven far out into the Mediterranean. Over a period of at least two weeks they were driven and tossed so violently that it appeared that the ship and all those aboard would sink. In an attempt to save the ship and themselves, along the way the crew threw out both the freight and the baggage that was on the ship. Still about to founder, they next tossed out the extra sails, rope, and tackle. As a last resort they finally threw the grain overboard (Acts 27:18-19, 38).

Finally the ship was driven aground and began to break up. (Acts 27:41) At this point, the Roman soldiers, knowing that they would be executed if any of the prisoners escaped, announced their intention of killing them all. Once again however, the centurion's respect for Paul is revealed. Seeking to spare Paul's life, he forbade the execution of any of the prisoners. That decision involved a significant risk on his part.

Eventually, however, all those on board the ship made their way safely to shore, where they were greeted by the inhabitants, who had apparently been watching the ship from the shore as it broke up and sunk (Acts 27:44b–28:2). At that initial meeting, the survivors discovered that they were on the island of Malta. Though the storm had cost them the loss of everything but their lives, they were hundreds of miles farther along on their way to Rome. However, they at last recognized that sailing was finally over for the season, leaving them with no choice but to spend the winter where they were, on Malta.

As we might have expected, while they were there, Paul filled his time with ministering to the inhabitants of Malta (Acts 28:7-10). Once again we find Paul being treated as someone significant. Even though a prisoner, he was welcomed by Publius, the ruler of the island. Publius has been identified outside the Bible by an inscription found on Malta.[9] Publius welcomed the centurion and possibly a few others of the passengers along with Paul and his companions to his palace. Paul was clearly not being treated as an ordinary prisoner. During their three-month stay on Malta, Paul, the centurion, and their companions discovered that there were other people wintering there from another ship. This second ship had apparently made it safely that far before the winter storms began. This ship was also a part of Rome's Alexandrian fleet, so the centurion would have been able to order the captain to allow his troops and prisoners to sail on it whenever it departed. They spent three months on Malta, waiting for the winter storms to pass, which brought Paul his companions to late winter, in the early part of AD 61.

We may surmise that, since this second ship was also a grain ship, its crew was obviously hoping to depart at the earliest possible moment. The possibility of high profits makes people take great risks. The ship is identified as having a figurehead of Castor and Polux, two minor Greek gods. Since this was so, the centurion and the owner of the grain may have superstitiously assumed that the date of the annual festival dedicated to these gods would be a propitious time for sailing. This festival occurred in late January each year.[10]

The second ship obviously departed from Malta earlier than would normally have been considered safe, for following their departure, they sheltered frequently along the way. However, following a brief and uneventful trip, they arrived at Rome's major passenger port, Puteoli (Acts 28:11-13). This would probably have been in February AD 61. If their cargo were handled as such cargo was normally treated, after disembarking the passengers at Puteoli, the ship would have proceeded northward to Ostia where the grain and other goods would have been off-loaded onto smaller vessels which then would have sailed up the Tiber into the city of Rome itself.

Regardless of the cargo, Paul and his companions disembarked at Puteoli and found Christians there. That Christians were there should not be

---

[9]Emil G. Kraeling, *I Have Kept the Faith* (New York: Rand McNally & Co., 1965) 247.
[10]Kraeling, *I Have Kept the Faith*, 248-49.

considered surprising, for with a major congregation at Rome—as reflected by Paul's letter—we would have expected that there would be a related congregation at Rome's major seaport. However, that they were numerous enough for Paul to locate them or for them to locate Paul may be surprising. Nonetheless it happened.

Paul was allowed by the Roman centurion to visit with the Christians at Puteoli for a week. This is just one more indication of the special treatment Paul was accorded by the Roman commander. Such a visit possibly held up all the soldiers and their other prisoners. At the very least it would have required the centurion to leave soldiers behind as a guard for Paul. After the week, however, those who had remained behind with Paul finally resumed their journey, eventually arriving at Rome a few days later, probably in early March AD 61 (Acts 28:14-16).

We can only imagine the emotions Paul felt as he finally approached and then entered the great city of Rome. For many years it had been the object of his longing. At long last he had arrived at what had clearly been the ultimate goal of his entire ministry (Rom. 1:9-10).

Rome—and Afterwards

When Paul arrived in Rome, he came as a prisoner, awaiting a trial before Caesar's tribunal. Since he was only an accused and not a con-demned prisoner, during this period of waiting he was allowed to live in his own house, accommodations which he had to rent for himself. During this extended period Paul was basically free to do anything that he wished ex-cept leave the house. Furthermore, during this time he would have had a soldier with him, a guard who probably would have had to be tied or shackled to Paul at all times (Acts 28:16). Such an arrangement would quite likely have necessitated two or more Roman soldiers living with him, so that they could have had some time off duty. Also, Paul probably was still accompanied by some of his friends. Paying for the cost of his dwelling and the food he and his companions consumed would have been no insignificant expense, an expense which had to be borne by Paul. Here is one more indi-cation that by this time in his life he was a man of some independent means.

In Rome, Paul could not begin his ministry by going to the Jews, as was his customary missionary strategy. In fact, he obviously could not go to anyone. However, he did ask the Jews to come to him, seeking even as a prisoner to maintain as much of the normal pattern of his ministry as was possible.

Not unexpectedly, the Jews of Rome had already heard of Paul. However, they had apparently heard nothing about his arrest and imprisonment in Judea, for they did not treat him as an enemy (Acts 28:21-22). In addition, they were quite aware that the Christian way was spoken against by their brothers in Jerusalem and throughout the Diaspora. They were certainly aware of the problems that earlier Christian missionaries in Rome had caused them.[11] Apparently after an initial meeting with his Jewish brothers, Paul made an opportunity to preach to them. He had the same kinds of results that he had experienced elsewhere in his ministry. While some of the Jews believed his message, others rejected it outright (Acts 28:24).

Again, following his normal pattern, upon his rejection by the Jews, Paul turned to the Gentiles of Rome. A Christian congregation was already in existence in the city, giving him an immediate base for operations. Many of its members were people with whom Paul had ministered in previous years. Others were people of whom Paul had heard. He had sent greetings to numbers of these, by name, when he had earlier written a letter to the Roman church from Corinth (Rom. 16:3-15).[12]

While awaiting his trial, Paul ministered to and through the Christians of Rome. At long last, he was doing what he had planned to do since some time before he had written his epistle to them: preaching the Gospel to the people who were in Rome (Acts 28:30-31; Rom. 1:15).

At this point, Luke's narrative about Paul comes to an abrupt end. The abrupt end may have been due to any number of reasons. First, something may have happened to Paul so that this part of the narrative came to a natural end. However, if this is true, we must wonder why Luke did not at least refer to whatever happened. Second, the abrupt ending may have been due to the fact that Luke intended to write a third scroll, similar to the first two (Luke and Acts). Third, Luke may even have written the third scroll, but somehow it has been lost, leaving us simply hanging at the end of this part of Paul's life and ministry. We need to remind ourselves that the Gospel of Luke leaves off after the resurrection of Jesus but before His ascension. Fourth, the abrupt ending may have been due to the fact that

---

[11]See the discussion in chapter 5 concerning the troubles in Rome during the reign of Claudius that had forced Aquila and Priscilla to leave Rome for Corinth.

[12]Many commentators deny that Paul wrote the last chapter of Romans because it is missing in some manuscripts. However, it sounds so much like Paul that we see no reason for not accepting it as having come from him, even if it were added later to a second or edited version of the epistle.

Luke was interrupted, either by his own death or by his own imprisonment. For whatever cause, the narrative we have in Acts simply stops. We can only surmise what happened to Paul during the remainder of his imprisonment and afterward, following the end of the story in Acts. Let us consider the possibilities.

We can be almost certain that if Paul did not fall sick and die, he finally had his hearing before Caesar's tribunal at the end of the two years of waiting. The fact that Luke was so precise in giving the detail that Paul spent "two whole years" under house arrest appears to make it abundantly clear that in some way this period of waiting came to an end. Furthermore, if at the end of those two years Paul had died of natural causes, Luke could hardly have ignored reporting a piece of information that significant. So Luke seems to have known that the years of Paul's Roman imprisonment had finally come to an end.

We can almost be just as sure that Paul had his hearing before Caesar's courts and was released. Luke was writing to a man by the name of Theophilus who was obviously a Roman and most likely a person of some significance (Luke 1:1-4; Acts 1:1). Throughout his narrative, Luke went to great lengths to show that on every occasion where Paul was brought before Roman officials to face charges of any kind, *he was never found guilty of any charge*. The Beloved Physician made this especially clear in writing about the years that followed Paul's arrest at the temple in Jerusalem. If he had ultimately been found guilty before Caesar's tribunal, stressing all of this would have been utterly pointless. If Theophilus were an important Roman, he would certainly have known the outcome of Paul's trial in Rome. Luke was trying to make it plain that no Roman had ever either found Paul guilty or Christianity seditious.

Therefore if Paul were tried and freed by Caesar's tribunal, what happened to him afterwards? Where did he go? What did he do? The answers to these questions can at best only be educated guesses. However, we do have a number of clues which may help us arrive at a more or less tentative conclusion concerning these issues.

Paul had expressly told the Romans in his epistle to them that he intended eventually to go to Spain, carrying the Gospel there (Rom. 15:24). The very fact that he had such intentions is evidence to some degree that he believed it was God's will for him to do just that. Further, if, as it appears likely, Paul wrote Philippians from Rome, he told his beloved friends in Philippi that, "I trust in the Lord that shortly I myself shall come [to you]" (Phil. 2:24).

We have no way of knowing whether either of these plans was ever fulfilled. Knowing Paul's twofold desire of always pressing on to new goals while at the same time maintaining contact with old friends, it is possible and perhaps likely that he ultimately accomplished both of these things. The Philippian evidence at least indicates that Paul expected to be released from his Roman imprisonment.

However, we must face the fact that if Paul were freed in the spring of AD 63, he would hardly have had time to go both to Spain in the west and Philippi in the east and be back in Rome to be executed by Nero in the persecutions of AD 64. Yet early traditions universally hold this to be true. Admittedly, traditions are not historical evidence. But since the traditions are without contradiction and also sound quite probable, they must at least be considered. However, if as some suggest Paul was not executed until the latter part of the 60s, both goals could quite easily be fitted into that period.

We must ask the question whether we have any evidence whether or not either of these goals, Spain and Philippi, was attained. The answer is a resounding, "Yes!"

First of all, the epistle to Titus gives us some evidence that must be considered. We have already raised the question as to whether 1 and 2 Timothy and Titus were actually written by Paul. One of the reasons offered for denying them to Paul is the fact that they contain geographical and ministerial references that cannot be fitted into Paul's ministry as recorded in Acts. However, if Paul were released from his Roman imprisonment and went on with his missionary purposes, these references can be fitted quite well into the years that followed the Acts narrative.

In the epistle to Titus, Paul said to his companion in ministry, "I left you in Crete, that you might amend what was defective" (Tit. 1:5). Furthermore, Paul urged Titus, "Do your best to come to me at Nicopolis, for I have decided to spend the winter there" (Tit. 3:12). While there were a number of cities named Nicopolis in the Roman empire, the one that appears most likely to have been intended by this reference was a port located in the province of Epirus, on the western border of the province of Macedonia. Philippi was located on the eastern edge of Macedonia. The only reason for Paul's being at Nicopolis would be if he were on his way to Philippi but had refrained from crossing the intervening mountains during the winter season.[13]

---

[13]Note that such geographical references as found here in Titus would make no sense

Second, as we have noted above, the traditions of the early church give evidence of Paul's release from his first Roman imprisonment and of a ministry to Spain which followed that release. As early as AD 90, Clement of Rome wrote that Paul had preached at the western extremity of the empire. He wrote this from Rome and the only significant land west of Rome was Spain. In addition, the Muratorian Canon from the early third century AD reflects the tradition of Paul's ministry in Spain. Further, Eusebius, an eminent early church historian, writing in the early part of the fourth century AD said that Paul was released from his first Roman imprisonment but was arrested and martyred following Paul's second visit to the city. (While he made no mention of a visit to Spain, he clearly knew of two separate Roman imprisonments.) Finally, in the fifth century AD both Jerome and Chrysostom refer to a mission by Paul in Spain.[14]

Admittedly, none of these references from the early church can be considered positive evidence of a visit by Paul to Spain as such. However, they do present a stream of tradition pointing to his release from the first Roman imprisonment and of a subsequent mission to Spain. The question is, where does this leave us in trying to reconstruct Paul's life and ministry?

If we are correct and Paul was released from house arrest following an appearance before Nero's tribunal, this would have occurred in the spring of AD 63. If so, he almost certainly departed for Spain as soon thereafter as possible and spent the summer months presenting his Gospel there. We have no indication of the outcome of that mission. However, since we find no traditions in Spain of Pauline churches there and since any visit there appears to have been brief, we may assume that he met with little or no success. Furthermore, his recurring health problems, aggravated by advancing age, may have forced him to cut short that mission and to have headed for Philippi in the early fall of AD 63.

---

if Paul had not put them there himself or if the author who was honoring Paul by writing it had not *known* that such references were actually a part of the apostle's ministry which were known by the people in the churches of the region. Either way, they reflect valuable evidence as to Paul's ministry following his first Roman imprisonment.

[14]Numerous others of the church fathers also accept the tradition of Paul's visit to Spain. Cf. F. L. Cross and E. A. Livingstone, *The Oxford Dictionary of the Christian Church*, 2nd ed. rev. (Oxford: University Press, 1983) 1047b; 3rd ed. (1997) 1235a; and Jack Finegan, "Spain," *The Interpreter's Dictionary of the Bible* (Nashville: Abingdon Press, 1962) R-Z: 430b.

As usual, Paul probably would have been accompanied on that entire journey by some of his companions in ministry, Titus being one of them. Further, either going to or coming from Spain he and his companions apparently made a visit to Crete. Following a brief and apparently successful ministry there, he left Titus behind and took his other companions with him as he continued his mission. This would have eventually led him to turn toward Philippi.

Such a journey to Philippi would have most likely put Paul ashore at Nicopolis just before the onset of the winter in AD 63. The threat and fear of winter snows in the mountains would have necessitated a continuing stay there. In AD 64, as he had purposed, he probably journeyed to Philippi and sometime thereafter returned to Rome. He may have been arrested on his way to Philippi or while he was there. However, it again appears that the balance of probability would indicate that Paul turned back toward Rome on his own, believing that this city which was the center of the empire was also the ultimate goal of his life and mission.

In any case, near the end of AD 64 Paul was back in Rome. If he had not been arrested earlier, he was most certainly arrested and imprisoned shortly after his arrival. That imprisonment would probably have been quite different from his first. This one was under close confinement, very rigorous, and quite brief. The rigor of this second confinement is indicated by the fact that Onesiphorus had to hunt for Paul and, after finding where he was, had a difficult time even getting to see him (2 Tim. 1:16-17). This second imprisonment also seems to have made Paul acutely aware that this time he could expect no release. As a result, he wrote to Timothy, his faithful companion and dear friend, saying:

> For I am already on the point of being sacrificed; the time of my departure has come. I have fought the good fight, I have finished the race, I have kept the faith. Henceforth there is laid up for me the crown of righteousness, which the Lord, the righteous judge, will award to me on that Day. (2 Tim. 4:6-8)

These are the words of a man who knows that his death is not only near; it appears to be inescapable.

Paul's second imprisonment was most likely a part of Nero's great persecution, started because he blamed the Christians for the great fire of Rome as an attempt to direct the hostility of the angry Roman citizens away from himself. This time Paul's release would certainly have been only by execution. So Paul was ultimately executed by the violent and irrational wrath of an angry and frightened emperor, seeking to appease an even more angry people.

At the end of His life, Jesus had been the Lamb of God (John 1:29, 36) Paul, on the other hand, became the scapegoat of Nero.

Writings from Rome

During Paul's first—or only—imprisonment in Rome, he had time both to think and to write. At this time he turned his mind back to the churches and the people who had figured so largely in his life. Also during this imprisonment he came across the runaway slave of his old friend, Philemon. When Paul had led the runaway slave Onesimus to faith in the Lord Jesus, Paul sent him home along with a letter reminding his old friend of past spiritual debts and recommending leniency and forgiveness.

Further, during this imprisonment, or possibly during the second and harsher imprisonment, Paul wrote to the beloved congregation in Philippi. No book in the Bible is so overflowing with the breath of joy as this one. His every thought of that congregation brought happy images to his mind and joy to his heart. They were the ones who again and again had ministered to his needs. And it was to them that he sent the greetings of the hardy saints of Caesar's household (Phil. 4:22). Consider the courage and faith of these people who dared to be Christians while serving in the very household of that beast in human form, Nero.

Also from the days of his first Roman imprisonment seem to have come Paul's letters to Colossae, to Laodicea (which has been lost, see Col. 4:16), and to the churches of Asia, a letter which apparently has been preserved for us as Ephesians. These letters were not brought forth by problems within the churches, as were most of his earlier ones. To the contrary, these letters sprang from a heart filled with precious memories and a mind concerned with the physical and spiritual trials that they were about to have to endure. As we have noted earlier, some people theorize that Paul had a time of imprisonment in Ephesus and place these letters as coming from that time. It is wholly unnecessary to invent an imprisonment of which we do not know when they fit in so well with an imprisonment of which we already know. Others place these letters as having come from the period of imprisonment in Caesarea. However, the references just do not seem to fit this period. Further, if Paul wrote the pastorals himself, 1 Timothy is most likely to be placed at this period of his life.

Finally, if we are correct in suggesting a release and a second Roman imprisonment, Titus would have been written during his winter stay at

Nicopolis between the two imprisonments. On his final return to Rome, his second imprisonment would have probably been brief and not afforded the ease of sending and receiving letters that his first one did. To this second imprisonment we would assign the other pastoral epistle, 2 Timothy, with its words of farewell to his son in the ministry. If there were no second imprisonment, then the pastoral letters, if genuine, must be assigned to the latter days of his only Roman imprisonment.

Some time late in AD 64, following the great fire of Rome, Paul suffered the fate of becoming a sacrificial victim of Nero. He who had urged others in Rome to be a living sacrifice and who had set them an example by his life, finally set the ultimate example of pouring out his own blood for the sake of his faith in the Lord Jesus (Rom. 12:1).

Paul had longed to go to Rome (Rom. 1:10-11, 13, 15). So at last he did. Paul had also longed to go to be with his Lord (Phil. 1:23). And so at last he did.

Chapter 8

Conclusion: Paul's Significance

At the beginning of this study I described Paul as a truly "great" man—
"*great* in every sense of the word and by almost every standard of
measurement that might be applied." As we have journeyed together
through Paul's life and ministry, I hope you have come to discover for
yourself what makes Paul so remarkable and worthy of our study. Perhaps
you have even come to share my assessment of Paul as *great*.

The focus of this study has been the history of Paul's life and ministry,
not the doctrinal content of his writings. We have examined the man and
how he carried out what he understood to be God's mission for him, more
than the theology Paul preached. This reflects both my concern with
keeping this volume of manageable length and the fact that Paul's teachings
have been extensively analyzed elsewhere. Many of what I consider to be
the best sources are listed in the bibliography.

But Paul's message is certainly a critical part of what made him great.
One of the most striking things about Paul is that you cannot spend long
studying his life without encountering that message. He truly practiced what
he preached, so we inevitably learn a great deal about Paul's faith and his
understanding of God's message by examining his actions. This is also part
of what makes Paul great. In fact, it is no exaggeration to say that Paul's
greatness is reflected in many aspects of his life and ministry—too many to
review in detail here. Six of those aspects, however, impress me as most
important and most relevant to this study. We will conclude by examining
those and seeing what they teach us about Paul's life and work, his
significance for Christianity, and his faith.

Paul the Educated Man

As already noted, more than one-third of the entire New Testament is
by, dedicated to, or about Paul. This sheer weight of words makes Paul
significant. No person in the New Testament, other than Jesus himself, has
more words devoted to him. However, it is not the weight of words about
him but the weight of his words that makes Paul significant.

Of all the leaders of the early church, Paul was obviously the best educated and the most intellectual. As we have discussed, he had been trained
as a rabbi, an extremely rigorous and demanding form of education.[1] Paul

---

[1]H. J. Schoeps, *Paul: The Theology of the Apostle in the Light of Jewish Religious
History*, trans. Harold Knight (Philadelphia: Westminster, 1961) 37-40, offers a brief but

studied in Jerusalem under Gamaliel and became a Pharisee (Acts 22:3; 23:6) So Paul would have had to master both Aramaic, the Jewish language of the day among the citizens of Jerusalem, and Hebrew, the language of the Jewish Scriptures. He also would have had to master the content of those Scriptures. In addition, he knew the rabbinic oral traditions, what later would be written down as the Babylonian Talmud, the Jerusalem Talmud, and the Palestinian Talmud.

We also know that he had a very good education in Greek—not just the language, but the literature and rhetorical forms as well. His knowledge of Greek language included the classical Greek of antiquity, the Greek of Aristotle and Plato, and *koine* ("common") Greek, the Greek of the ordinary person. This allowed Paul to communicate with people throughout the northeastern Mediterranean world without the need for translators.

Paul's Greek education also allowed him to draw on Greek dramatists, philosophers, and poets. He quotes from several such that we can identify specifically. Luke reports that in his Areopagus speech Paul quotes both Epimenides—"In him we live and move and have our being"—and Aratus—"For we are indeed his offspring" (Acts 17:28). From Meander Paul quoted, "Bad company ruins good morals" (1 Cor. 15:33). Titus 1:12 again quotes Epimenides: "Cretans are always liars, evil beasts, lazy gluttons." Paul's mastery of philosophers at Athens shows great familiarity both with their ideas and with their methods and approaches to dealing with the great issues of life (Acts 17:16-31).

It is also interesting to note that Paul quoted Greek writers in the same terms that he used when he quoted the Old Testament. For Paul, an educated man, all truth was God's truth wherever he found it.

Paul also demonstrates considerable familiarity with the stoic philosophy for which his home town of Tarsus was famous. Whether or not he received formal training in stoicism, in his letters he uses the imaginary dialogue, the rhetorical questions, the irony of stoic debate. He adopted its moral earnestness, its humanitarian spirit, and its interest in the deep things of the soul.

Paul thus brought to his ministry and his writings the best of religious and secular education. He not only had a rich store of knowledge and

excellent survey of the nature of rabbinic training in the first century and carefully notes its influences upon Paul. Without question, this aspect of Paul's life was influential upon his spirituality, his knowledge of the Hebrew Scriptures, and his commitment to serious and thorough thought.

experience, but also knew how to use it. He knew how to think about the material he had learned. He was no parrot, but an original thinker. In every aspect, he truly deserved to be called an educated man. This sets Paul apart from other New Testament authors and early church leaders. It also undoubtedly contributed to Paul's success and to his lasting influence.

Paul the Missionary

In addition, from the standpoint of the Christian church, Paul was clearly the most effective missionary and evangelist among the first disciples. From the moment of his conversion he sought to spread the Gospel. Luke writes that, upon his conversion, "immediately he [Paul] began to proclaim Jesus" (Acts 9:20 NRSV). More than this, however, he was among the very first missionaries that any church or group of Christians purposefully sent out to carry the Gospel to regions where no one knew it and to people who had never heard of Jesus Christ. His was no accidental witness but an intentional sharing of the message of Jesus with those who had never heard.

Furthermore, he regularly chose the most difficult people to whom to tell his story, doing it eagerly and skillfully. It was Paul who began intentionally to establish Gentile churches, earning for himself the title of "the apostle to the Gentiles." It was Paul who faced down those who thought that all Christians must first become Jews (Acts 15).

Paul was remarkably strategic in how he undertook his missionary efforts. Murphy-O'Connor writes:

> Given the limited time available (Paul expected that Christ would return shortly in glory) and the vastness of the world, it was clear to Paul that he could not afford to fritter away his energies by stopping at any town or village just because it happened to lie on his path, or by accepting any invitation that happened to be offered. He needed places that, in addition to absorbing his message, had the capacity to radiate it out.[2]

The New Testament provides many examples of Paul bypassing a small or poorly located town for a provincial capital or major trading city located near a port or significant roads (see Acts 13:4-6, 14; 16:8). Paul's ministry, like his background, was essentially urban in focus. He preached in places sufficiently large and well located to ensure a sizable audience of listeners

---

[2]Jerome Murphy-O'Connor, *Paul: His Story* (Oxford: Oxford University Press, 2004) 70.

who could carry the Gospel to other parts of the world that he would never personally visit.[3] Paul was a missionary's missionary.

It is also important to recognize that a major feature of Paul's mission work was his sense that what he did or did not do was always guided by God's Holy Spirit. "So, being sent out by the Holy Spirit" (Acts 13:4). "And they went through the region of Phrygia and Galatia, having been forbidden by the Holy Spirit to speak the word in Asia" (Acts 16:6). "And when they had come opposite Mysia, they attempted to go into Bithynia, but the Spirit of Jesus did not allow them" (Acts 16:7). Paul's considerable education and experiences never blinded him in his search for God's will. Quite the contrary, they helped Paul perceive and act on the direction of the Holy Spirit.

Paul the Church Planter

The third aspect of Paul's extraordinary significance for the early church was his emphasis on starting churches. In modern days, we are used to an emphasis being placed on "church planting" and "church planters." For Paul, however, this was an innovation, and it was a task to which he devoted his life. In spite of, and in addition to, all his other accomplishments, Paul was preeminently a church planter. He went places where there were no churches, in fact, he went where there were no Christians, and left behind him new churches when he departed. They were not always thriving and were never perfect. But they were there.

When he came to the end of his life, churches existed all over the northeastern end of the Mediterranean world as testimony to his vitality and effectiveness as a missionary-evangelist and church planter. Those churches are in a very real sense the spiritual footprints of the great apostle.

The Importance of Membership. Why did Paul start churches? I believe the answer is found in his understanding of Christians as members of the "body of Christ." This is not just a metaphor. Paul is one of the earliest people we know to call a person a "member" of anything. Up until Paul, a "member" was a term of anatomy. The finger is a member of the hand. The hand is a member of the body. The eyes are members of the head. So when Paul called believers members of the body of Christ he meant that the relationship between individual believers and Christ was the same as

---

[3]The cities in which Paul ministered are described in detail in Richard Wallace and Wynne Williams, *The Three Worlds of Paul of Tarsus* (London: Routledge, 1998) 153-222.

between individual parts of the anatomy and the body. "Now you are the body of Christ and individually members of it" (1 Cor. 12:27).

For Paul, however, membership in the body not only described the relationship of individuals to Christ, but also the relationship among individual members. "There may be no discord in the body, but that the members may have the same care for one another. If one member suffers, all suffer together; if one member is honored, all rejoice together" (1 Cor. 12:25-26).

For Paul it was necessary—it was absolutely essential—for a Christian to be active in a congregation of believers, in the body of Christ. This conviction stressed the equality of all Christian believers. This was critical in light of the ongoing debate in the early church, prompted by the Judaizers, about whether Gentiles had to convert to Judaism before becoming Christians. "For by one Spirit we were all baptized into one body—Jews or Greeks, slaves or free—and all were made to drink of one Spirit. For the body does not consist of one member but of many" (1 Cor. 12:13-14).

The importance of membership also emphasized the important contributions and the fundamental interdependence of each individual.

> If the whole body were an eye, where would be the hearing? If the whole body were an ear, where would be the sense of smell? But as it is, God arranged the organs in the body, each one of them, as he chose. If all were a single organ, where would the body be? As it is, there are many parts, yet one body. The eye cannot say to the hand, "I have no need of you," nor again the head to the feet, "I have no need of you." (1 Cor. 12:17-21)

Membership was not a choice for Paul. A Christian could no more say that he was not a member of the body of Christ than a foot or eye could say it was not a member of the human body: "that would not make it any less a part of the body" (1 Cor. 12:15, 16).

The word Paul uses most frequently in his writings is the Greek preposition meaning "together with." We translate it most often as "fellow." Paul uses this word to describe Christians as "fellow athletes," "fellows in burial of baptism," "fellow components of a buildings," "fellows corporate blended together in one body," "fellows in death," "fellows in groaning," "fellows in the heavenlies," "fellow heirs," "fellows in life," "fellow partakers," "fellow refreshed," "fellow rejoicing," "fellow servants," "fellow soldiers," "fellow sympathizers," "fellow workers," "fellow built," "fellow citizens," "fellow comforters," "fellow contenders," "fellow crucified," "fellows in glory," "fellow growing," "fellow helpers," "fellow imitators," "fellow minded," "fellow prisoners," "fellow reigning with Christ," "fellow risen," "fellow sharers," "fellow sufferers," "fellow travailers," "yokefellows," and even as "fellows in fellowship."[4]

Perhaps the most heartrending words we find in any of Paul's letters are those to Timothy describing his trial in Rome: "No one took my part; all deserted me" (2 Tim. 4:16). Paul deeply believed in the essential "fellowship" of Christianity. Churches were the practical manifestation of this fellowship.

It is interesting to note how much Paul's convictions about Christian fellowship were influenced by his Old Testament understanding of corporate personality. No Hebrew would ever have said, "What I do does not affect anybody but me." The Hebrews knew their actions affected everyone else. They knew it, Paul knew it, and it contributed to his life's work founding churches. Recall that all of Paul's letters, except for those to Timothy and Titus, the authenticity of which has been questioned, are addressed to communities of believers, not to individuals.

Church Organization. Paul is significant not only for the central role that Christian fellowship—membership—played in his understanding of the Gospel, or for the number of churches he started, but also for the structure he gave those churches. That structure has had a lasting impact on Christianity.

Paul seems to have patterned the churches he started after the Jewish synagogue. For example, Paul created *independent* churches. Although linked in fellowship with other churches, they were not subservient. They were distinct communities of believers. The word Paul uses for "church," *ekklesia*, was used to describe "the citizens of a free Greek city officially assembled for self-governmental decisions."[5] The connection to a free community of believers is unmistakable.

It is instructive to consider how Paul identified himself in his letters to churches. He does not describe himself as their founder or as a representative of another congregation. Instead he referred to himself as, for example, "called by the will of God to be an apostle of Christ Jesus" (1 Cor. 1:1); "an apostle of Christ Jesus by the will of God," (2 Cor. 1:1); and "a servant of Jesus Christ, called to be an apostle, set apart for the gospel of God" (Rom.

---

[4]White, *Apostle Extraordinary*, 107.
[5]Crossan and Reed, *In Search of Paul*, 165-66.

1:1). In his letter to the churches in Galatia he is even more explicit: "Paul an apostle—not from men nor through man, but through Jesus Christ and God the Father, who raised him from the dead" (Gal. 1:1).

Also like synagogues, churches did not have permanent pastors or rabbis. Rather, it was the responsibility of all members to learn and develop and teach. So Paul could say, "Having gifts that differ according to the grace given to us, let us use them" (Rom. 12:6). It was a fundamental precept of Paul's faith that Christians required no other intermediary other than Jesus. All believers—and all churches—were fundamentally equal: "since all have sinned and fall short of the glory of God, they are justified by his grace as a gift, through the redemption which is in Christ Jesus" (Rom. 3:23-24).

Paul's understanding of the church as formed by equals, however much the members might differ in social or financial status in other walks of life, was vividly demonstrated in his instructions to the church at Corinth concerning the Lord's Supper. Unlike in modern times, the Lord's Supper in the early church was a real meal, shared by the members of the church. Eating together was—as it often still is—an important part of fellowship, but in the first century it inevitably posed many issues. For example, could Jews and Gentiles eat together in the face of the rigid dietary laws followed by the former?

First-century meals posed another problem as well. Typically, the master of the house, his family, and honored guests would eat at one table. Friends of a lower order would not only eat at another table, but they ate different food as well. Servants would eat still different food at a third table.

What happened when the church, which might very well have members from all three groups and more, met to commemorate the Last Supper? The church at Corinth had developed a practice whereby everybody brought their own food, thus effectively perpetuating the stratification that existed outside of the church. Paul sharply criticized this practice: "When you meet together, it is not the Lord's supper that you eat. For in eating, each one goes ahead with his own meal, and one is hungry and another is drunk" (1 Cor. 11:20-21).

Instead, Paul instructed the church: "So then, my brethren, when you come together to eat, wait for one another—if any one is hungry, let him eat at home—lest you come together to be condemned" (1 Cor. 11:33-34). A proper understanding of the Lord's Supper requires that all share together equally. For Paul, the church could not tolerate inequality among believers.

With the exceptions of his letters to Timothy and Titus, there is "not the slightest hint . . . that Paul ever left anyone in charge of the communities he founded."[6] Those churches certainly had leaders. Paul, in fact, specifically provided for the selection of elders (bishops) and deacons (1 Tim. 3:1-13; Tit. 1:5-9). But these were provided by churches from within their own membership, not imposed from outside. The Greek word Luke uses when he describes Paul and Barnabas "appointing" elders means "to choose by a show of hands" (Acts 14:3). The churches Paul founded appointed their own leaders. Moreover, Paul consistently addressed himself to churches in their entirety, for example, "To all the saints in Christ Jesus who are at Philippi, with the bishops and deacons" (Phil. 1:1).

Just as each believer was a member of the body of Christ, so was each church. So while churches might be physically separate, they each bore Christian responsibility for each other. "Bear one another's burdens, and so fulfill the law of Christ" (Gal. 6:2). Paul arranged for the churches in Galatia, Corinth, and Macedonia to contribute to support the needs of impoverished Christians in Jerusalem (1 Cor.16:1-3; 2 Cor. 8:1-7). Paul himself journeyed to Jerusalem on at least three occasions to consult with other church leaders (Gal. 1:18-20; Rom. 15:25-32; 1 Cor. 16:1-4), and to address the doctrinal dispute over whether Gentiles must first become Jews before accepting Jesus (Gal. 2:1-10).

Paul believed that all churches shared a responsibility for missions. As a result, even though one church may have been created as the "mission" of another, not only was the new church not subservient to the old, but it had its own mission responsibilities (2 Tim. 4:1-5). Paul thought of the church, consistent with most of his beliefs, in extremely activist terms.

Paul the Preacher/Teacher

The fourth area of Paul's significance for the early church rests in his ability as a preacher/teacher. I connect these even though the two disciplines have unfortunately been separated by many contemporary pulpiteers. The reason I connect them is the fact that they were certainly not separated in the practice of the early church. The preaching of the first century church clearly included both of the disciplines of teaching and preaching. Good preaching still should. Good exhortation is always based upon solid

---

[6]Crossan and Reed, *In Search of Paul*, 118.

teaching. And the church's teaching should always lead to the presentation of the divine demands made upon its pupils.

Any serious student of the New Testament is quite aware of the commonalities of all the sermons in the book of Acts, whether they are purported to come from Peter, Stephen, or Paul. Without demanding that in every recorded sermon of Paul we have his actual words, what we clearly do have, at the very least, is a serious tradition that he was an excellent preacher.

Further, the responsiveness of audiences to Paul's proclamation, as reflected in Acts, lends support to the assertion that he was an excellent preacher. An ineffective proclamation would never have stirred up the riots and opposition that Paul's preaching did. He was remembered as one of the more effective preachers of the early Christians by both his friends and enemies. Acts also gives us, at the very least, a tradition as to the content of the sermons which he preached. They were remembered as being representative of mainline *kerygma*, the proclamation of the church's good news about Jesus.[7]

Paul the Theologian

A fifth area in which Paul's contribution to the early church was of significance is that of theology. In fact, so great was his significance here that many contemporary interpreters have asserted that the early church's memory of Jesus has been seriously altered and enlarged by the writings of Paul. Without debating that issue at this point, we may note that the theological sections of Paul's epistles present the clearest development of a faith statement to be found among any of the New Testament writers (with the possible exception of the author of Hebrews).

Paul's epistle to the church at Rome still stands as the greatest exposition of the nature of the Christian faith ever produced. Martin Luther called Romans "the chief book of the New Testament and the purest Gospel." He wrote that "the Christian should not only have every word of Romans by heart, but should take it about with him every day as the daily bread of his

---

[7]Ralph P. Martin, *New Testament Foundations: A Guide for Christian Students*, vol. 2, *Acts–Revelation* (Exeter: Paternoster Press; Grand Rapids MI: Eerdmans, 1978) 76-77, gives a brief discussion and a fruitful footnote relating to both the strengths and weaknesses of assuming that all of the sermons in Acts follow the same "kerygmatic" outline. At the very least, the similarity of the sermons in Acts shows a basic consistency in the approach of the early church in presenting the Gospel to their world.

soul."[8] Samuel Taylor Coleridge described Romans as "the most profound work in existence."[9] In *The Interpreter's Bible*, John Knox called Romans "unquestionably the most important theological book ever written."[10]

This high praise is only a sampling of that accorded to Romans by a diverse range of commentators. It is not within the scope of this study to explore Paul's theology in Romans in any detail. However, no discussion of Paul's significance would be complete without considering at least briefly the key elements of his letter to the church at Rome.

Romans is the only letter that Paul wrote to a church he had not previously visited. In a very real sense, it is an introduction of Paul to the church at Rome and a declaration of his desire to visit there (Rom. 1:1-15; 15:23-24, 28). Romans reflects an effort by Paul to establish a common bond with the church at Rome. Paul attempts this in part by identifying twenty-five members of the church by name, three house churches, and two groups of slaves or former slaves (Rom. 16:1-15).

Paul seeks to create that bond with the church at Rome primarily, however, by addressing an issue with which he had had much experience and that he believed to be of common concern. That issue was the relationship of Jews and Gentiles with each other and with Christ. The process of explaining this, however, necessarily required Paul to expound a more complete theology about the relationship of God and man.

Paul summarizes the core of that theology in one sentence: "[The Gospel] is the power of God for salvation to every one who has faith" (Rom. 1:16). Because all have sinned, all require salvation—Jews and Gentiles alike. That salvation comes from God, as a gift of sheer grace, manifest in the life and sacrifice of Jesus Christ:

> But now the righteousness of God has been manifested apart from law, although the law and the prophets bear witness to it, the righteousness of God through faith in Jesus Christ for all who believe. For there is no distinction; since all have sinned and fall short of the glory of God, they are justified by his

---

[8]Martin Luther, "Preface to the Epistle to the Romans" (1522), in *Works of Martin Luther* (1932) 6:447.

[9]Samuel Taylor Coleridge, *The Table Talk and Omniana of Samuel Taylor Coleridge*, ed. Coventry Kersey Dighton Patmore (Oxford/New York: Oxford University Press, 1917) 232.

[10]John Knox (introduction and exegesis) and Gerald R. Cragg (exposition), "The Epistle to the Romans," in *The Interpreter's Bible* 9:355-668 (Nashville: Abingdon Press, 1954) 355a.

grace as a gift, through the redemption which is in Christ Jesus, whom God put forward as an expiation by his blood, to be received by faith. This was to show God's righteousness, because in his divine forbearance he had passed over former sins. (Rom. 3:21-25)

The Old Testament concept of God's grace meant the "unmerited favor" of God that we do not deserve and have no right to expect. The Greek word for "grace" is *charis* and might more literally be translated as "free gift." "You do not earn it, deserve it, or gain it by any personal or even communal effort. But you do have to accept it."[11] The believer accepts God's grace—his free gift—through faith. "Faith does not mean intellectual consent to a proposition, but vital commitment to a program. . . . total dedication . . . a total lifestyle commitment."[12]

Paul returns to this theme again and again: all have sinned and nothing man can do on his own—no amount of obedience to Old Testament law—can restore man's relationship with God. But God has reached out to man through Jesus, who died for our sins, so that anyone who has faith in—or, more accurately, is faithful to—that salvation and accepts Jesus as Lord is restored to God's favor:

> Therefore, since we are justified by faith, we have peace with God through our Lord Jesus Christ. Through him we have obtained access to this grace in which we stand, and we rejoice in our hope of sharing the glory of God. . . .
>
> While we were still weak, at the right time Christ died for the ungodly. . . . But God shows his love for us in that while we were yet sinners Christ died for us. Since, therefore, we are now justified by his blood, much more shall we be saved by him from the wrath of God. For if while we were enemies we were reconciled to God by the death of his Son, much more, now that we are reconciled, shall we be saved by his life. Not only so, but we also rejoice in God through our Lord Jesus Christ, through whom we have now received our reconciliation. . . .
>
> . . . For the wages of sin is death, but the free gift of God is eternal life in Christ Jesus our Lord. (Rom. 5:1-2, 6, 8-11; 6:23)

It is impossible to miss Paul's wonder at the magnificence and power of God's "free gift" to humanity of salvation and eternal life (Rom. 5:15-16; 6:23). "We rejoice in our hope of sharing the glory of God. . . . Not only so, but we also rejoice in God through our Lord Jesus Christ, through whom we

---

[11]Crossan and Reed, *In Search of Paul*, 73.
[12]Crossan and Reed, *In Search of Paul*, 385-86.

have now received our reconciliation" (Rom. 5:2, 11). Paul was always overwhelmed at what God had done for him that he did not deserve at all.

Having accepted God's remarkable gift, Paul writes in Romans, the kingdom of God that lies ahead is "righteousness and peace and joy in the Holy Spirit" (Rom. 14:17). We need to be very clear here. Paul was no mindless optimist. He was not suggesting that the believer will not face "tribulation, or distress, or persecution, or famine, or nakedness, or peril, or sword" (Rom. 8:35). He certainly faced most or all of these during his ministry. Rather, for Paul, none of these hardships—not even death itself—can compare with the certainty of God's love and grace: "No, in all these things we are more than conquerors through him who loved us" (Rom. 8:37).

> For I am sure that neither death, nor life, nor angels, nor principalities, nor things present, nor things to come, nor powers, nor height, nor depth, nor anything else in all creation, will be able to separate us from the love of God in Christ Jesus our Lord. (Rom. 8:38-39)

These were not idle words. Paul knew what he was talking about. During his ministry, as we have seen, five times Paul was flogged with thirty-nine lashes; three times he was beaten with rods; once he was stoned; three times he was shipwrecked. During his missionary journeys he had been in frequent "danger from rivers, danger from robbers, danger from my own people, danger from Gentiles, danger in the city, danger in the wilderness, danger at sea, danger from false brethren." He had endured "toil and hardship, through many a sleepless night, in hunger and thirst, often without food, in cold and exposure" (2 Cor. 11:24-27).

Nevertheless, he could write in Romans that "in all these things we are more than conquerors through him who loved us" (Rom. 8:37).

> What then shall we say to this? If God is for us, who is against us? He who did not spare his own Son but gave him up for us all, will he not also give us all things with him? (Rom. 8:31-32)

The magnitude of God's "free gift" is not only a subject of conviction and awe for Paul, it also transforms the lives—and necessarily the actions— of believers. Paul twice quotes a passage from the Old Testament book of Habakkuk: "He who through faith is righteous shall live" (Rom. 1:17; Gal. 3:11; Hab. 2:4). Interestingly, there is no word for "faith" in the Old Testament. The word in the Old Testament is "faithfulness." Believers are righteous by *being faithful*.

Paul spends most of the last five chapters of Romans describing what it means to be faithful. Commentators sometimes describe this section of

Romans as the "Christian ethic"—the standards by which Christians should live.

> I appeal to you therefore, brethren, by the mercies of God, to present your bodies as a living sacrifice, holy and acceptable to God, which is your spiritual worship. Do not be conformed to this world but be transformed by the renewal of your mind, that you may prove what is the will of God, what is good and acceptable and perfect. (Rom. 12:1-2)

Paul identified many duties of believers, but these might be summarized in two of his admonitions: "Love one another with brotherly affection" (Rom. 12:10); and "Do not be overcome by evil, but overcome evil with good" (Rom. 12:21). Paul's concern is not with creating laws; salvation is not through obedience to the law or good works, but through faith alone. Rather, Paul is identifying those behaviors by which believers may demonstrate their faithfulness, and help themselves and each other grow in Christian maturity. We demonstrate what we believe by what we do.

Such a short and selective summary of course does not do justice to Paul's remarkable statement of Christian faith. But it at least gives an indication of the power of Paul's message and the utter conviction and joy with which he shared it with the church at Rome and throughout his ministry.

Paul the Convert

Paul's enthusiasm in Romans suggests the final area of Paul's significance for the church of the first century and of today: that of convert. Although Paul never called himself a "convert" or described his Damascus Road experience as a "conversion," it was clearly his transformation on that journey from Jerusalem to Damascus that made all the difference in his life. That experience transformed the persecuting opponent of Christianity into the proclaiming proponent of the Lord Jesus. Paul wrote to the churches of Galatia:

> For you have heard of my former life in Judaism, how I persecuted the church of God violently and tried to destroy it; and I advanced in Judaism beyond many of my own age among my people, so extremely zealous was I for the traditions of my fathers. (Gal. 1:13-14)

Paul's conversion turned his extreme zealousness from "persecuting the church of God violently"—what the New American Standard Bible translates as "beyond measure"—to proclaiming the Gospel of the Lord Jesus Christ. It also transformed the one who was the leader of those who sought

to destroy the early church into the one who became the leader of those who
sought to spread that same church and its Gospel throughout the world.

The fact that Paul was a convert was hardest for both believers and
unbelievers to accept and understand. And this added the greatest depth to
his significance for the early church. The transformation of Paul was not
only unexpected, it was unbelievable to friend and foe alike.[13]

Paul's conversion underlay all of his actions and teachings. C. S. Lewis
described his conversion experience in a book with the title *Surprised by
Joy*. Paul might have applied the same title to his conversion. In fact, the
second most frequently used word in his letters is a preposition which, when
used with the accusative case, means "over and above" or "excessive." To
put it in a modern idiom, it means "super."

Paul believed that everything in Christianity was super. This is reflected
in his actions, especially his far-flung missionary trips. It is also reflected,
as we have seen, in his writings. Paul was unabashed in his energy and
enthusiasm for the Gospel, what R. E. O. White has described as a
"ceaseless pageant of triumph."

> Paul's [reaction to God's grace] was one of boundless and wondering
> gratitude. The secret of Paul, as W. C. Piggott has said, "the real clue to all his
> labours is not to be found in his arguments, but in his doxologies, his outbursts
> of pure wonder at the grace of God, or of almost heartbreaking glory in the
> cross of our Lord Jesus Christ."[14]

Paul's enthusiasm was only intensified by the urgency, even impatience, he felt in the face of the impending return of Jesus Christ: "the night
is far gone, the day is at hand" (Rom. 13:12). "Forgetting what lies behind
and straining forward to what lies ahead, I press on toward the goal for the
prize of the upward call of God in Christ Jesus" (Phil. 3:13-14).

The boundless energy, enthusiasm, and single-minded commitment of
the convert, "straining forward to what lies ahead," are the most distinctive
characteristics of Paul's ministry. They were the standards by which he
judged himself. When he wrote to Timothy from imprisonment in Rome,
"I have fought the good fight, I have finished the race, I have kept the faith"
(2 Tim. 4:7), the Greek word he used for faith conveys a total preoccupation

---

[13]Alan F. Segal so emphasizes this point that he has written an entire book on the
subject: *Paul the Convert* (New Haven CT: Yale University Press, 1990).

[14]White, *Apostle Extraordinary*, 31.

with "remaining faithful to one's word, loyal and completely committed."[15] It requires a commitment to "put out the utmost effort."[16] This undoubtedly helps to explain the remarkable success of Paul's ministry and his legacy in the church. It may be his most important lesson for Christians throughout time.

[15]Jerome D. Quinn and William C. Wacker, *The First and Second Letters to Timothy: A New Translation with Notes and Commentary*, Eerdmans Critical Commentary (Grand Rapids MI: Eerdman's, 2000) 777.

[16]James D. G. Dunn, "The First and Second Letters to Timothy and the Letter to Titus," *The New Interpreter's Bible* 11:773-880 (Nashville: Abingdon Press, 2000) 856.

Glossary

agora—The Greek word for "market" or "marketplace," *agora* describes the open space near a city's gates where business and community life were centered. In Athens, it was also the place where public debates and lectures were held.

allegorical method—A method of interpreting Scripture used by many rabbis of the New Testament era, popularized particularly by Philo of Alexandria. Totally ignoring any context or historical background, such a method allowed the interpreter to identify each and every feature of a narrative with any spiritual feature which the interpreter desired. Such a method allowed any passage to mean anything desired by the interpreter.

amanuensis—From the Latin "at/by hand," a professional secretary or scribe. At times they apparently wrote at their master's dictation. At other times, they seemingly had great freedom in recording the thoughts of the one whom they served.

anit-Semitism, anti-Semitic—A term describing attitudes and actions hostile or detrimental to the Jewish people, based upon the prejudice of the one opposed to them. Anti-Judaism.

Antonia (Tower of)—A tower fortress at the northwest end of the Temple court, originally built by David, restored by the Maccabees, and eventually enlarged by Herod the Great. During the New Testament era, it was used by the Romans as a barracks for their troops quartered in Jerusalem.

Apocrypha (of the Old Testament)—The fourteen books related to the Old Testament which are accepted as (deutero)canonical by Roman Catholics and others but are deemed noncanonical as Scripture by Protestants, Evangelicals, and Jews. They were a part of the Septuagint from which Jereome's Latin Vulgate was made but were never a part of the Hebrew Scriptures.

apologetic writings—Writings done with the express purpose of defending either a person or an idea.

apostle—Originally this word meant "one who has been sent." In the early church it quickly came to refer to the original Twelve whom Jesus selected as his special emissaries, with the addition of Paul.

Aramaic—The everyday language of the Jewish people of Palestine during the New Testament era, derived from ancient Hebrew.

Artemis—An Ephesian goddess identified with the Roman goddess Diana. She was considered to be the goddess of wild nature and her worship

was related to the fertility cults of the mother goddess found throughout
the ancient Near East, being highly sexual.

Caesar's tribunal—The official place or places of judgment in Rome where
the courts of Caesar rendered decisions.

Castor and Pollux—Ancient ships usually had figures carved into their
prows, normally depicting some god or spirit who was the protector of
the ship. Castor and Polux were two minor Greek gods who were so
used on the ship by which Paul eventually arrived in Italy.

Church Fathers—Christian writers of the late first and early second century
AD who supposedly had known the apostles.

Cilician Gates—The major mountain pass through the Taurus Mountains,
this was a narrow gorge cut by a tributary of the river Cydnus. It served
as the passage for a trade route between Mesopotamia and Asia Minor.[1]

Cypriot—An an inhabitant or a native of the island of Cyprus.

Damascus Document—The only nonbiblical text found among the Dead
Sea Scrolls which was known before their discovery, also known as the
Zadokite Document. The manuscript describes the faith of a sect of
Judaism established long after the Babylonian exile, frequently
identified as the Essenes.

Dead Sea Scrolls—The popular name given to a collection of Jewish
manuscripts found in the western hills above the Dead Sea. They
contain many manuscripts of Old Testament books, as well as other
manuscripts from the sect which created and preserved them at ancient
Qumran.

devout—In the Jewish terminology of the time, a "devout" Gentile was one
who worshipped the God of Israel without actually having become a
convert to Judaism. Identical to "God-fearer" (see especially Acts 10:2,
then Acts 10:22; 13:16, 26).

Diaspora—Refers to those Jews who had been scattered around the
Mediterranean world as refugees or captives, or because of business and
commercial interests. The longer they had been away from the land of
Israel as such, the more they had assimilated Judaism with the religion
and philosophy of the places where they lived.

elders—Originally a technical term referring to the older people of any
community and by New Testament times specifically referring to the

---

[1]See Charles F. Pfeiffer and Howard F. Vos, *The Wycliffe Historical Geography of
Bible Lands* (Chicago: Moody Press, 1967) 314, 316, 317, 339-40.

older people in a synagogue. The early church seems to use the term either to refer to the older members of any church or to those in a congregation who have been Christians longest.

epistle—A technical term for ancient Greek correspondence. Some interpreters make a difference between ordinary letters and the more formal epistles. No such distinction is made here.

Feast of Unleavened Bread—One of the three great pilgrim feasts of Judaism, this was joined with Passover to remind Israel of their deliverance from Egypt.

Gamaliel—A highly influential rabbi who was a Pharisee and a member of the Sanhedrin during the time Christianity was first beginning. He was the teacher under whom Paul studied.

Hellenists—Derived from the Greek word *hellas*, which was their name for their own land, this term refers to Jewish people who believed that they should adopt a Greek way of life.

Jerusalem Council—Also identified as the Jerusalem Conference. This gathering of the leaders of the churches in Jerusalem and Antioch debated the issue of whether or not a Christian must first be a Jew before becoming a Christian (reported in Acts 15).

Judaizers—Jewish people who proclaimed a belief that no one could be a Christian without first becoming a Jew.

kerygma—The transliteration of a Greek word meaning "proclamation." Since the time of C. H. Dodd, it has come to refer specifically to the content or outline of the sermons found in the Book of Acts, believed to typify those things which the early church felt were necessary to be in any proclamation about Jesus to their contemporaries.

koine—The common Greek language spoken and understood by ordinary people throughout the Roman empire in the time of Paul. This was not the highly developed, elegant language of classical Greek but the ordinary language of the common people. This is the language in which the New Testament was written.

Levite—A descendant of the Jewish tribe of Levi. Levites were the only ones allowed to serve in the Temple worship. By New Testament times, it seems to refer to the Temple singers or choir members.

LXX—Abbreviation for Septuagint, the best-known Greek translation of the Old Testament. So designated because of the tradition that the translation was accomplished by 72 translators in 72 days. (The traditional 72 was rounded to 70, LXX.)

Messiah—A technical Jewish term for the "anointed one" of God who would ultimately come to bring about the deliverance of the Hebrew people.

Nazirite—From the Hebrew word, *nazir*, meaning "vow." A Nazirite was one who had made a special vow to God. Upon the completion of the vow, specially prescribed offerings had to be made to signify that the vow had been fulfilled.

Passover—The primary religious festival of the Jews, celebrating their deliverance from Egypt at the time of the Exodus. It was the first among the great pilgrim feasts, when Jews came to Jerusalem from all over the empire.

Pauline—An adjective describing events, concepts, ideas, or books related to Paul.

Pentecost—Literally "the fiftieth day" and referring to the Feast of Weeks which celebrated the beginning of harvest, *fifty days* after Passover.

Pharisees—A religious-political party of the Jewish people in the first-century AD. They sought a strict observance of the Law of the Old Testament. They were a harsh, highly disciplined people, but extremely moral.

Philo—A Jewish philosopher of Alexandria, born shortly before Jesus. His writings sought to combine Greek thought and philosophy with historic Judaism, with the intent of popularizing Judaism among the philosophers of his day. His major approach to the Jewish scriptures was allegorical.

politarchs—The official title of the rulers of Thessalonica, indicating the city's considerable autonomy within the Roman empire.[2]

Praetorian Guard—The personal guards attached to any Roman governor or emperor. As used here, we confine it to those attached to the emperor himself, thus the imperial guard.

proconsul—A technical term referring to the governor of a senatorial province in the Roman government. Such a person was technically responsible to the Roman Senate.

Procrustean bed—This expression comes from an ancient Greek legend of a king who had a bed in which any person would fit. If they were too short, they were stretched to fit. If they were too tall, their feet and legs

---

[2]*Mercer Dictionary of the Bible*, 910.

were cut off. This term is applied to those who alter evidence to make it fit their presuppositions.

procurator—A governor of a small Roman province who was appointed directly by the emperor rather than by the Senate.

pseudepigrapha—Letters or other writings in the name of a master or teacher other than the actual author, reflecting the teachings or traditions of that master or teacher.

Q—A adopted by New Testament scholars as an abbreviation of the German word *Quelle*, "source." It refers to a supposed source of material Matthew and Luke have in common but which are not found in any of the other Gospels. Such material appears to have been a collection of the teachings of Jesus.

Qumran—The ancient site around which the Dead Sea Scrolls were found. It may either have been a Jewish fortress, an Essene monastery, or perhaps even both but at separate times.

rabbi—A person trained in the interpretation and exposition of the Hebrew Scriptures, with particular emphasis upon the Law (Torah). In the first-century AD, synagogues did not normally have a rabbi specifically attached to them. When such trained persons visited a synagogue, they were given an opportunity to read and expound on the Scriptures.

Sadducees—A Jewish religious party active in the New Testament era which was primarily made up of the wealthy aristocracy and which emphasized collaboration with their foreign overlords in order to maintain the peace and their own power. They would not collaborate in matters of what they deemed to be ultimate issues of faith, but these were few and far between. Contrary to the Pharisees, they did not believe in any form of life after death.

Sanhedrin—The official high court and chief legislative body of Judaism. To be a member, a man had to be at least thirty years old and had to be married. Paul may have been a member of this group, in which case this a vital clue to his age and marital status.

Septuagint—The name of the best-known Greek translation of the Hebrew Scriptures. It means "seventy" and is abbreviated by the Roman numeral LXX. It seems to have been the text used by the early Christians who were scattered around the Mediterranean world. Tradition has it that it was the product of 72 rabbis being given 72 copies of the Hebrew Bible and told to translate the text into Greek, which they accomplished in 72 days. (See LXX, above.)

synagogue—A local congregation of Judaism where the Jews gathered to worship God and to study their scriptures. These sprang up all around the empire wherever there were enough Jewish people to form and support one.

Theophilus—The person to whom both the Gospel of Luke and the Book of Acts were addressed.

Torah—The Hebrew word for Law (or Instruction) which describes both the Hebrew Scriptures and the legal requirements of their Scriptures. Also the designation of the section Genesis–Deuteronomy in the Hebrew Bible.

Bibliography

General Works

Adams, Edward. *Constructing the World: A Study in Paul's Cosmological Language.* Edinburgh: T.&T. Clark, 2000.

Africa, Thomas W. *The Immense Majesty, A History of Rome and the Roman Empire.* New York: Crowell, 1974. Repr.: Arlington Heights IL: AHM Publishing Corporation, 1974; and Arlington Heights IL: Harlee Davidson, 1974, 1991.

Babcock, William S., ed. *Paul and the Legacies of Paul.* Dallas: Southern Methodist University Press, 1990.

Baly, Denis. *The Geography of the Bible.* New York: Harper & Brothers Publishers, 1957.

Barclay, William, ed. *The Bible and History.* London: Lutterworth Press, 1968.

Barrett, C. K. *Paul. An Introduction to His Thought.* London: Geoffrey Chapman, 1994. Louisville: Westminster/John Knox Press, 1994.

Becker, Jürgen. *Paul: Apostle to the Gentiles.* Translated by O. C. Dean, Jr. Louisville: Westminster/John Knox Press, 1993.

Beker, J. Christiaan. *Heirs of Paul.* Edinburgh: T.&T. Clark, 1992.

Best, Ernest. *Paul and His Converts.* Edinburgh: T.&T. Clark, 1988.

Blaiklock, E. M. "The Acts of the Apostles as a Document of First Century History." *Apostolic History and the Gospel: Biblical and Historical Essays Presented to F. F. Bruce on His 60th Birthday.* Edited by W. Ward Gasque and Ralph P. Martin. Exeter: Paternoster Press, 1970.

Bruce, F(rederick). F(yvie). *Paul and Jesus.* London: SPCK, 1977.

_____. *Paul: Apostle of the Free Spirit.* Exeter: Paternoster Press, 1977.

_____. *This Is That.* London: Paternoster Press, 1968.

Buckmaster, Henrietta. *Paul: A Man Who Changed the World.* New York: McGraw-Hill Book Company, 1965.

Caird, G. B. *The Apostolic Age.* London: Gerald Duckworth & Co., Ltd., 1955.

_____. "Chronology of the New Testament." *The Interpreter's Dictionary of the Bible* A–D:599-607. Nashville: Abingdon Press, 1962.

Callaway, Joseph A. "Corinth." *Review and Expositor* 57 (October 1960).

Cate, Robert L. *A History of the Bible Lands in the Interbiblical Period.* Nashville: Broadman Press, 1989.

_____. *A History of the New Testament and Its Times.* Nashville, Broadman Press, 1991.

_____. *Old Testament Roots for New Testament Faith.* Nashville: Broadman Press, 1982.

Christensen, Duane L. "Chronology," *Mercer Dictionary of the Bible*, 147-50. Macon GA: Mercer University Press, 1990.

Ciholas, Paul. "Epistle/Letter." *Mercer Dictionary of the Bible*, 258. Macon GA: Mercer University Press, 1990.

Cross, F. L., and E. A. Livingstone, editors. *The Oxford Dictionary of the Christian Church*. Second and revised edition. Oxford: University Press, 1983; ^{2}1974; ^{1}1957. Third edition, edited by E. A. Livingstone, 1997.

Crossan, John Dominic, and Jonathan L. Reed. *In Search of Paul*. New York: HarperSanFrancisco, 2004.

Cullmann, Oscar. *The Early Church: Studies in Early Christian History and Theology*. Abridged edition. Philadelphia: Westminster Press, 1966.

Dibelius, Martin. *The Book of Acts: Form, Style, and Theology*. Edited by Kenneth C. Hanson. Fortress Classics in Biblical Studies. Philadelphia: Fortress Press, 2004. This is a revised edition (with updated documentation) of Dibelius's *Studies in the Acts of the Apostles*. Edited by Heinrich Greeven. Translated by Mary Ling. London: SCM Press; New York: Scribner's, 1956.

Dibelius, Martin, and Werner Georg Kummel. *Paul*. Philadelphia: Westminster Press, 1953.

Donaldson, Terence J. *Paul and the Gentiles*. Minneapolis: Fortress Press, 1997.

Dowley, Tim, editor. *Eerdman's Handbook to the History of Christianity*. Grand Rapids MI: William B. Eerdmans Publishing Co., 1977.

Elden, Bastiaan Van. "Some Archaeological Observations on Paul's First Missionary Journey," *Apostolic History and the Gospel: Biblical and Historical Essays Presented to F. F. Bruce on His 60th Birthday*. Edited by W. Ward Gasque and Ralph P. Martin. Exeter: Paternoster Press, 1970.

Filson, Floyd V. *A New Testament History*. London: SCM Press, 1964.

Finegan, Jack. *A Handbook of Biblical Chronology*. Princeton NJ: Princeton University Press, 1964.

_____. "Spain." *The Interpreter's Dictionary of the Bible* R–Z:429-30. Nashville: Abingdon, 1962.

Fisher, Fred L. *Paul and His Teachings*. Nashville: Broadman Press, 1974.

Glover, T. R. *Paul of Tarsus*. London: SCM, 1927.

Goodwin, Frank J. *A Harmony of the Life of St. Paul*. Grand Rapids MI: Baker Book House, 1951.

Grant, Michael. *Saint Paul*. London: Weidenfeld and Nicolson, 1976.

Grollenberg, L. H. *Atlas of the Bible*. Translated by Joyce Reid and H. H. Rowley. London: Thomas Nelson and Sons Ltd., 1965.

Hengel, Martin. *Acts and the History of Earliest Christianity*. Translated by John Bowden. London: SCM Press, 1979.

_____. *Jews, Greeks, and Barbarians*. London: SCM Press, 1980.

_____. *The Pre-Christian Paul*. Translated by John Bowden. London: SCM Press, 1991.

Heyer, C. J. den. *Paul: A Man of Two Worlds*. Translated by John Bowden. Harrisburg PA: Trinity Press International, 2000.

Horsley, Richard A., editor. *Paul and Empire: Religion and Power in Roman Imperial Society*. Harrisburg PA: Trinity Press International, 1997.

Hovhannessian, Vahan. *Third Corinthians: Reclaiming Paul for Christian Orthodoxy*. New York: Peter Lang, 2000.

Hunt, E. W. *Portrait of Paul*. London: A. R. Mowbray & Co. Ltd., 1968.

Hunter, Archibald M. *Paul and His Predecessors*. Philadelphia: Westminster Press, 1961.

Hurd, J. C. "Chronology, Pauline." *The Interpreter's Dictionary of the Bible* supplementary volume, 166-67. Nashville: Abingdon, 1976.

Jagersma, Henk. *A History of Israel from Alexander the Great to Bar Kochba*. Translated by John Bowden. London: SCM Press, 1985; Philadelphia: Fortress Press, 1985.

Jervell, Jacob. *The Unknown Paul: Essays on Luke-Acts and Early Christian History*. Minneapolis: Augsburg Publishing House, 1984.

Jewett, Robert. *A Chronology of Paul's Life*. Philadelphia: Fortress Press, 1979.

_____. *Dating Paul's Life*. London: SCM Press Ltd, 1979.

Keppler, Thomas S. *Contemporary Thinking about Paul*. Nashville: Abingdon-Cokesbury Press, 1940.

Kraeling, Emil G. *I Have Kept the Faith*. New York: Rand McNally & Co., 1965.

Leaney, A. R. C. *The Jewish and Christian World: 200 B.C. to A.D. 200*. Cambridge: Cambridge University Press, 1984.

Lentz, John Clayton, Jr. *Luke's Portrait of Paul*. Cambridge: Cambridge University Press, 1993.

Lohse, Eduard. *The First Christians: Their Beginnings, Writings, and Beliefs*. Translated by M. Eugene Boring. Philadelphia: Fortress Press, 1983.

_____. *The New Testament Environment*. Translated by John E. Steely. Nashville: Abingdon Press, 1976.

Luedemann, Gerd. *Paul, Apostle to the Gentiles: Studies in Chronology.* Philadelphia: Fortress Press, 1984.

Lyons, George. *Pauline Autobiography*. Atlanta: Scholars Press, 1985.

Malina, Bruce J. *The New Testament World*. Atlanta: John Knox Press, 1981.

_____, and Jerome H. Neyrey. *Portraits of Paul*. Louisville: Westminster/John Knox Press, 1996.

Martin, James. *The Empty Tomb*. New York: Harper & Brothers, 1960.

May, Herbert G., editor. *Oxford Bible Atlas*. Third edition. New York: Oxford University Press, 1984.

Mellink, M. J., "Tarsus," *The Interpreter's Dictionary of the Bible* R–Z:518-19. Nashville: Abingdon Press, 1962.

Meyers, Eric M., and James F. Strange. *Archaeology, the Rabbis, and Early Christianity*. London: SCM Press, 1981.

Mills, Watson E., et al., editors. *Mercer Dictionary of the Bible*. Macon GA: Mercer University Press, 1990.

Murphy-O'Conner, Jerome. *Paul and Qumran*. London: Geoffrey Chapman, 1968.

_____. *Paul: A Critical Life*. Oxford: Clarendon Press, 1996.

_____. *Paul: His Story*. Oxford: Oxford University Press, 2004.

Ogg, George. *The Chronology of the Life of Paul*. London: Epworth Press, 1968.

Park, Eung Chun. *Either Jew or Gentile*. Louisville: Westminster/John Knox Press, 2003.

Perowne, Stewart. *The Political Background of the New Testament*. London: Hodder, 1958.

Pfeiffer, Charles F., and Howard F. Vos. *The Wycliffe Historical Geography of Bible Lands*. Chicago: Moody Press, 1967.

Ramsay, William Mitchell. *St. Paul the Traveler and the Roman Citizen*. The Morgan Lectures 1894. London: Hodder and Stoughton, [1]1895. Repr. from the 1926 edition: Grand Rapids: Baker Book House, 1982.

Reicke, Bo. *The New Testament Era: The World of the Bible from 500 B.C. to A.D. 100*. Translated by David E. Green. Philadelphia: Fortress Press, 1964.

Robinson, John A. T. *Redating the New Testament*. London: SCM Press, 1976.

Roetzel, Calvin J. *Paul: The Man and the Myth*. Columbia: University of South Carolina Press, 1998.

Russell, D. S. *From Early Judaism to Early Church*. London: SCM Press, 1986.

Sampley, J. Paul, editor. *Paul in the Greco-Roman World*. Harrisburg PA: Trinity Press International, 2003.

Schoeps, H. J. *Paul: The Theology of the Apostle in the Light of Jewish Religious History*. Translated by Harold Knight. Philadelphia: Westminster Press, 1961.

Schürer, Emil. *The History of the Jewish People in the Age of Jesus Christ (175 B.C.–A.D. 135)*. Three volumes. Revised edition. Translated by T. A. Burkill et al. Revised and edited by Geza Vermes and Fergus Millar. Edinburgh: T.&T. Clark, 1973–1986.

Segal, Alan F. *Paul the Convert*. New Haven CT: Yale University Press, 1990.

Sherwin-White, A. N. *Roman Society and Roman Law in the New Testament*. Oxford: Clarendon Press, 1963.

Silberman, Neil Asher. "The World of Paul." *Archaeology* (November/December 1996): 30-36.

Smith, James. *The Voyage and Shipwreck of St. Paul*. Fourth edition. London: Longmans, Brown, Green, Longmans, and Roberts, 1848.

Stalker, James. *Life of St. Paul*. New York: Fleming H. Revell, 1912.

Stewart, James Stuart. *A Man in Christ: The Vital Elements of St. Paul's Religion*. London: Hodder and Stoughton; New York: Harper & Brothers, 1935.

Tenny, Merrill C. *New Testament Times*. Grand Rapids MI: William B. Eerdmans Publishing Co., 1965.

Tidball, Derek. *The Social Context of the New Testament*. Grand Rapids MI: Acadamie Books, 1984.

Wallace, Richard, and Wynne Williams. *The Three Worlds of Paul of Tarsus*. London: Routledge, 1998.

Walton, Steve. *Leadership and Lifestyle: The Portrait of Paul in the Miletus Speech and 1 Thessalonians*. Cambridge: Cambridge University Press, 2000.

White, Reginald E. O. *Apostle Extraordinary*. Grand Rapids MI: William B. Eerdmans Publishing Co., 1962.

Whiteley, D. E. H. *The Theology of St. Paul*. Oxford: Basil Blackwell, 1964.

Wiles, Gordon P. *Paul's Intercessory Prayers*. Cambridge: Cambridge
    University Press, 1974.
Wilson, A. N. *Paul: The Mind of the Apostle*. London: Sinclair-Stevenson,
    1997.
Winter, Bruce W. *After Paul Left Corinth: The Influence of Secular Ethics
    and Social Change*. Grand Rapids MI: William B. Eerdmans Publishing
    Co., 2001.

New Testament Introductions

Freed, Edwin D. *The New Testament: A Critical Introduction*. Belmont,
    California: Wadsworth Publishing Company, 1991.
Guthrie, Donald. *New Testament Introduction*. Fourth edition. Downers
    Grove IL: Intervarsity Press, 1990.
Harrison, Everett F. *Introduction to the New Testament*. Grand Rapids MI:
    William B. Eerdmans Publishing Co., 1964.
Hunter, Archibald M. *Introducing the New Testament*. Third revised
    edition. Philadelphia: Westminster Press, 1972.
Johnson, Luke T. *The Writings of the New Testament*. Philadelphia: Fortress
    Press, 1989.
Kee, Howard Clark. *Understanding the New Testament*. Englewood Cliffs
    NJ: Prentice Hall, 1993.
Koester/Köster, Helmut. *Introduction to the New Testament*. Volume 1,
    History, Culture, and Religion of the Hellenistic Age. Volume 2,
    History and Literature of Early Christianity. Translated from the
    German (1980) by the author, Helmut Koester. Foundations & Facets:
    New Testament. Philadelphia: Fortress Press; Berlin/New York: Walter
    de Gruyter, 1982.
Lohse, Eduard. *The First Christians: Their Beginnings, Writings, and
    Beliefs*. Translated by M. Eugene Boring. Philadelphia: Fortress Press,
    1983.
Martin, Ralph. *New Testament Foundations*. Two volumes. Exeter:
    Paternoster Press, 1975, 1978.

Commentaries

Allan, John A. *The Epistle to the Ephesians*. London: SCM Press, 1959.
Barclay, William. *The Acts of the Apostles*. Second edition. Daily Study
    Bible. Philadelphia: Westminster Press, 1955.
_____. *The Letters to the Corinthians*. Second edition. Daily Study Bible.
    Philadelphia: Westminster Press, 1956.

_____. *The Letters to the Galatians and Ephesians.* Second edition. Daily Study Bible. Philadelphia: Westminster Press, 1958.

_____. *The Letters to Timothy, Titus, and Philemon.* Second edition. Daily Study Bible. Philadelphia: Westminster Press, 1960.

Best, Ernest. *The Letter of Paul to the Romans.* Cambridge Bible Commentary. Cambridge: Cambridge University Press, 1967.

Betz, Hans Dieter. "Christianity as Religion: Paul's Attempt at Definition in Romans." *Journal of Religion* 71/3 (July 1991): 315-44.

Boers, Hendrikus. *The Justification of the Gentiles: Paul's Letter to the Galations and Romans.* Peabody MA: Hendrickson, 1994.

Bruce, F(rederick). F(yvie). *The Acts of the Apostles: The Greek Text with Introduction and Commentary.* Third revised and enlarged edition. Grand Rapids: William B. Eerdmans Publishing Company, 1990.

_____. *Commentary on the Book of Acts. The English Text with Introduction, Exposition, and Notes.* The New International Commentary on the New Testament. Grand Rapids MI: William B. Eerdmans Publishing Company, 1954. Second edition, 1977. Revised edition, 1988.

Caird, G. B. *Paul's Letters from Prison.* Oxford: Oxford University Press, 1976.

Cragg, Gerald R. (exposition), and John Knox (introduction and exegesis). "The Epistle to the Romans." *The Interpreter's Bible* 9:353-668. Nashville: Abingdon Press, 1954.

Deming, Will. *Paul on Marriage and Celibacy: The Hellenistic Background of 1 Corinthians 7.* Cambridge: Cambridge University Press, 1995.

Dunn, James D. G. *The Theology of Paul's Letter to the Galations.* Cambridge: Cambridge University Press, 1993.

_____. "The First and Second Letters to Timothy and the Letter to Titus." *The New Interpreter's Bible* 11:773-880. Nashville: Abingdon Press, 2000.

Felder, Cain Hope. "The Letter to Philemon." *The New Interpreter's Bible* 11:881-905. Nashville: Abingdon Press, 2000.

Foakes-Jackson, F. J. *The Acts of the Apostles.* Moffatt New Testament Commentary. New York and London: Harper and Brothers, 1931.

Grayston, Kenneth. *The Letters of Paul to the Philippians and to the Thessalonians.* Cambridge Bible Commentary. Cambridge: Cambridge University Press, 1967.

Hanson, Anthony Tyrrell. *The Pastoral Letters.* Cambridge Bible Commentary. Cambridge: Cambridge University Press, 1966.

Hays, Richard B. "The Letter to the Galatians." *The New Interpreter's Bible* 11:181-348. Nashville: Abingdon Press, 2000.

Hooker, Morna D. "The Letter to the Philippians." *The New Interpreter's Bible* 11:467-550. Nashville: Abingdon Press, 2000.

Hunter, Archibald M. *The Epistle to the Romans*. London: SCM Press, 1955.

_____. *Interpreting Paul's Gospel*. Philadelphia: Westminster Press, 1954.

Johnson, Luke T. *The Acts of the Apostles*. Sacra Pagina 5. Collegeville MN: Liturgical Press, 1992.

Kern, Philip H. *Rhetoric and Galations: Assessing an Approach to Paul's Epistle*. Cambridge: Cambridge University Press, 1998.

Knox, John (introduction and exegesis), and Gerald R. Cragg (exposition). "The Epistle to the Romans." *The Interpreter's Bible* 9:353-668. Nashville: Abingdon Press, 1954.

Lincoln, Abdrew T. "The Letter to the Colossians." *The New Interpreter's Bible* 11:551-670. Nashville: Abingdon Press, 2000.

Litfin, Duane. *St. Paul's Theology of Proclamation: 1 Corinthians 1–4 and Greco-Roman Rhetoric*. Cambridge: Cambridge University Press, 1994.

Luthi, Walter. *The Letter to the Romans*. Translated by Kurt Schoenenberger. Richmond VA: John Knox Press, 1961.

Marshall, I. Howard. *Acts: An Introduction and Commentary*. Leicester: Inter-Varsity Press, 1980.

Mills, Watson E., et al., editors. *Mercer Commentary on the Bible*. Macon GA: Mercer University Press, 1994.

Mitchell, Margaret M. *Paul and the Rhetoric of Reconciliation: An Exegetical Investigation of the Language and Composition of 1 Corinthians*. Louisville: Westminster/John Knox Press, 1991.

Nanos, Mark D. *The Irony of Galations: Paul's Letter in First-Century Context*. Minneapolis: Fortress Press, 2002.

Neil, William. *The Letter of Paul to the Galatians*. Cambridge Bible Commentary. Cambridge: Cambridge University Press, 1967.

Packer, J. W. *The Acts of the Apostles*. Cambridge Bible Commentary. Cambridge: Cambridge University Press, 1966.

Perkins, Pheme. "The Letter to the Ephesians." *The New Interpreter's Bible* 11:349-466. Nashville: Abingdon Press, 2000.

Quinn, Jerome D. *The Letter of Titus: A New Translation with Notes and Commentary and an Introduction to Titus, I and II Timothy, the Pastoral Epistles*. Anchor Bible 35. New York: Doubleday, 1990.

_____, and William C. Wacker. *The First and Second Letters to Timothy.* Grand Rapids: William B. Eedrmans Publishing Co., 2000.

Ramsay, William Mitchell. *A Historical Commentary on St. Paul's Epistle to the Galatians.* In the *Expositor* (June 1898–September 1899). New York: G. P. Putnam's Sons, 1900. Repr.: Grand Rapids MI: Baker Book House, 1965.

Robertson, Archibald Thomas. *Word Pictures in the New Testament.* Volume 3, "The Acts of the Apostles." Nashville: Broadman Press, 1930.

_____. *Word Pictures in the New Testament.* Volume 4, "The Epistles of Paul." Nashville: Broadman Press, 1930.

Roetzel, Calvin J. *The Letters of Paul: Conversations in Context.* Second edition. Atlanta: John Knox Press, 1982.

Sampley, J. Paul. "The First Letter to the Corinthians." *The New Interpreter's Bible* 10:771-1004. Nashville: Abingdon Press, 2002.

_____. "The Second Letter to the Corinthians." *The New Interpreter's Bible* 11:1-180. Nashville: Abingdon Press, 2000.

Smith, Abraham. "The First Letter to the Thessalonians." *The New Interpreter's Bible* 11:671-738. Nashville: Abingdon Press, 2000.

_____. "The Second Letter to the Thessalonians." *The New Interpreter's Bible* 11:739-72. Nashville: Abingdon Press, 2000.

Thompson, G. H. P. *The Letters of Paul to the Ephesians, to the Colossians and to Philemon.* Cambridge Bible Commentary. Cambridge: Cambridge University Press, 1967.

Thrall, Margaret E. *The First and Second Letters of Paul to the Corinthians.* Cambridge Bible Commentary. Cambridge: Cambridge University Press, 1965.

Wall, Robert W. "The Acts of the Apostles." *The New Interpreter's Bible* 10:1-368. Nashville: Abingdon Press, 2002.

Wiles, Maurice F. *The Divine Apostle: The Interpretation of St. Paul's Epistles in the Early Church.* Cambridge: Cambridge University Press, 1967.

Wright, N. T. "The Letter to the Romans." *The New Interpreter's Bible* 10:393-770. Nashville: Abingdon Press, 2002.

Index of Persons

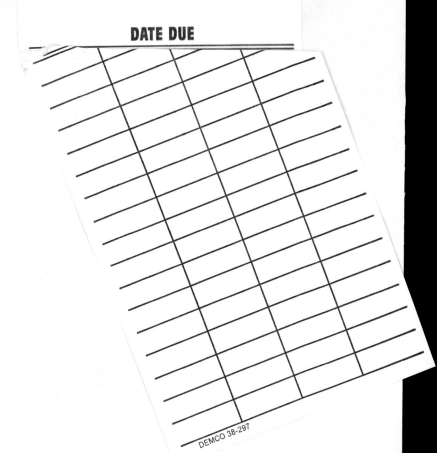

DATE DUE

DEMCO 38-297